THE FULSTOW BOYS

GORDON STEEL

Gordon Steel burst on to the theatre-scene with his first play, *Dead Fish*, which won a Fringe First Award at the 1993 Edinburgh Festival. It toured nationally and was the beginning of a fruitful relationship with Hull Truck Theatre. Since then, Gordon has written *Like A Virgin, Studs, A Pair Of Beauties, Albert Nobbs, Kissing Married Women, A Kick In The Baubles* and *Wilde Boyz* for Hull Truck Theatre. Gordon is also the author of *Jumping The Waves,* which was commissioned for the opening of the Arc Theatre. Gordon has worked extensively as a director, and directed the premieres of *Like A Virgin, A Pair Of Beauties, Dead Fish, Studs, Albert Nobbs* and *Kissing Married Women.*

For television, Gordon wrote *Cock And Bull,* which was included in the Channel Four Sitcom Festival. He is currently developing some new ideas for television, including an adaptation of *The Fulstow Boys.*

Gordon has set up his own theatre company, Steelworks, whose debut production, *Grow Up Grandad,* was produced at the ARC in 2015. In 2019 he was a Journal Culture Awards Writer of the Year finalist.

Gordon is a lifelong supporter of Middlesborough Football Club.

THE FULSTOW BOYS

by Gordon Steel

Based on a true story that happened in the town of Fulstow, Lincolnshire in 2005 and in the Great War.

JOSEF WEINBERGER PLAYS

LONDON

THE FULSTOW BOYS
First published in 2019
by Josef Weinberger Ltd
12-14 Mortimer Street, London W1T 3JJ
www.josef-weinberger.com / plays@jwmail.co.uk

ISBN: 978 0 85676 380 9

THE FULSTOW BOYS was first presented by *Steelworks Theatre Company* at ARC, Stockton-on-Tees on 5th September 2018. The cast was as follows:

NICOLA PIKE .... Laura Mould

CHARLES KIRMAN / TIM PIKE .... Joshua Hayes

FRANCIS KIRMAN / GRAHAM............................... Simeon Truby

GEORGE MARSHALL Snr / MAURICE....................... David Nellist

GEORGE MARSHALL Jnr / DANNY /
OLD MAN / MILITARY POLICEMAN .... Ash Matthews

DORA / MOIRA .... Katy Federman

Directed by Gordon Steel
Designed by Foxton
Assistant Director: Dani Arlington
Script Consultant: Rebecca Steel
Lighting Design: Tony Wilcock
Stage Manager: Alison Rigby-Roberts
Musical Arrangement: Andrew McIntyre

CHARACTERS

2005

NICOLA PIKE *(Early 40s)*
TIM PIKE *(Mid 30s – Nicola's husband)*
GRAHAM *(Early 50s)*
MAURICE *(Early 50s)*
MOIRA *(42)*
DANNY *(Early 20s)*
OLD MAN *(82)*

1914–1918

CHARLES (CHARLIE) KIRMAN *(Late 20s)*
DORA *(Mid 20s – Charles Kirman's wife)*
FRANCIS KIRMAN *(Late 40s – Charles Kirman's father)*
GEORGE MARSHALL Jnr *(16 – Son)*
GEORGE MARSHALL Snr *(Late 40s – Father)*
MILITARY POLICEMAN

It is possible, with the doubling up of roles, to perform the play with six actors:

NICOLA PIKE
CHARLES KIRMAN / TIM PIKE
FRANCIS KIRMAN / GRAHAM
GEORGE MARSHALL Snr / MAURICE
GEORGE MARSHALL Jnr / DANNY /
    OLD MAN / MILITARY POLICEMAN
DORA / MOIRA

For . . .

Rebecca for brilliant, insightful script notes.

Dani Arlington for being so supportive.

Glenda for all your administrative work.

Jack and Hannah for your constant love and support.

Annabel Turpin and ARC for their ongoing support.

*Ray Spencer and The Customs House
for believing in and backing the project.*

ACT ONE

Scene One

The set consists of a latched door SR. and a door SL. USC of the doors is a cutaway set of a wall and a window. To the right and left of this are placed sandbags. US of this is a cyclorama. Through the doors SR and SL we see the sandbags and the cyclorama. In front of the USC wall is a sideboard and in front of the sideboard is a trestle table. To the left of the sideboard is a small table. Wooden chairs are situated to the right of the SR door and to the left of the SL door. A small radiator sits to the left of the SL door behind the chairs. A group of sandbags are piled up DSR. They double up as a small seat.

August 1914. Music: Stanley Holloway – 'Lily of Laguna'. CHARLES, a young carefree man in his late twenties, enters quickly from the wings SL carrying DORA, fireman's-lift-style. DORA, laughing and kicking out her legs, struggles to break free as CHARLES spins her round.

DORA   Charlie, put me down. Charlie! Charlie, put me down.

CHARLES   Do you love me?

DORA   Put me down.

CHARLES   Say it. Say it.

DORA   Alright, alright, alright.

CHARLES   Say it.

DORA   I love you, I love you.

                (He stops swinging her and puts her down and starts singing over her dialogue.)

DORA   Don't do that again. I'm all dizzy. What would have happened if you'd dropped me? Then you wouldn't be laughing.

CHARLES   (*Singing, from 'Lily of Laguna'.*)
I know she likes me
I know she likes me
Because she said so.

DORA   By Charlie Kirman; you love yourself, you do.

CHARLES   You'll miss me when I'm gone.

DORA   Will I?

CHARLES   You'd better.

DORA   (*Teasing him.*) Ooooh, I don't know.

CHARLES   Right, well I'll have to give you something to make you miss me.

DORA   (*She backs off.*) No, Charlie.

CHARLES   Come here.

DORA   Charlie, you stop it now.

(*She turns and runs for it.* CHARLES *chases her.*)

Charlie, no. Charlie, Charlie.

(*He catches her and pins her to the ground.*)

Charlie, no.

(*He tickles her furiously. She screams with laughter attempting to wriggle free.*)

I'll miss you. I'll miss you. I promise. I'll miss you.

(*He releases her.*)

I can't breathe. Don't do that again.

(*There's a pause.* CHARLES *sits looking out over the fields of Fulstow.*)

Look at the state of me. You wanna keep your hands to yourself, Charlie Kirman, do you hear me? You could do me an injury, carrying on like that.

(*She becomes aware of* CHARLES *lost in thought. She sits next to him.*)

CHARLES	I love these fields. (*He sighs and sits and breathes in the open sky.*) I love a big sky. (*Pause.*) Do you think, right now there are Germans sat in a field talking about going to fight the English? You know, another couple like us.
DORA	There isn't another couple like us. (*Innocently.*) Where is Germany?
CHARLES	It's not far. Just across the North sea.
DORA	(*Panicking.*) Is it?
CHARLES	Yeah.
DORA	Oh God! Is it bigger than us?
CHARLES	I dunno.
DORA	I hope not. (*A beat.*) What are they like?
CHARLES	Germans?
DORA	Yeah.
CHARLES	Well, I've heard, they grow to fifteen feet tall, have a bone through their nose and talk funny. Just like people from Leeds.

DORA   (*She slaps him about the body.*) Why don't you
           talk proper to me?

CHARLES   I think they're much the same as us.

DORA   (DORA *pauses for a while but has another
           question that she is a little reluctant to ask.*)
           Sorry Charlie, but, why are we fighting them?

CHARLES   (*Unsure how to start.*) Well, it's like . . . well
           let's say someone hurt you.

DORA   Me? Why would anybody hurt me?

CHARLES   No, they wouldn't.

DORA   Well why did you say they would?

CHARLES   No, they wouldn't, it's just . . . Listen, just for
           the sake of argument, if someone did hurt you –
           which they're not – but if they did, they'd have
           me to reckon with, wouldn't they.

DORA   Aw, Charlie. (*From the back she puts her arms
           round him and snuggles up.*)

CHARLES   Well, it's a bit like that, with this war carry-
           on. Germany has been hurting our friends and
           we're not going to stand to see our friends get
           hurt are we?

DORA   No, we're not.

CHARLES   We're gonna do something about it, aren't we?

DORA   Yes, we are.

CHARLES   Well there you go.

DORA   (*Pause.*) But, I'm scared.

CHARLES   What are you scared of?

DORA   I don't know. It's just . . . well, what if
            something happened to you?

CHARLES   Me? Nothing's gonna happen to me. Me strong
            and muscley.

DORA   I'm serious. You know I couldn't bear to be
            without you, Charlie.

            (*They look at each other.*)

CHARLES   Look, I'm a Fulstow boy, there is no way I'm not
            coming back here.

DORA   Promise me.

CHARLES   I promise.

DORA   Because, if anything happened to you, well, I
            don't think *we* could cope on our own.

CHARLES   I've told you, don't you worry about – we?

            (DORA *is a bit coy.*)

            Dora!

            (*He looks at her, she is a little bit scared, unsure
            of his reaction. Pause. He stands.*)

            Are you serious? No, you couldn't be. It's not
            possible. Well it is possible? Are you?

            (*A smile escapes from* DORA.)

            Oh bloody hell, you are. Oh heck!

DORA   (*Pause.*) Are you happy, Charlie?

CHARLES   Happy! Happy! (*A mobile phone starts ringing.*)
            I'll show you happy, come here.

DORA   (*Backing off.*) No Charlie. Don't.

(NICOLA PIKE, *laden with bags and a microphone
stand, bursts through the SL door. The bags
contain stuff for the party; packets of balloons,
party poppers, squeakers, table cloths, plates,
cups, cutlery, etc. She carries one bag in her
mouth and speaks through gritted teeth.*)

NICOLA   Oh for fuck's sake. Bloody thing.

(DORA *shrieks and laughs as* CHARLES *pursues her
off.*)

Scene Two

NICOLA *starts to divest herself of the possessions she has amassed
for the fancy dress fundraising event, before throwing the lot on
the floor. She searches pockets and bags and finds her phone.
Just as she retrieves the phone and goes to answer it, it stops
ringing.*

NICOLA   Bloody thing. I'm warning you.

(*She collects up the bags and the microphone
stand once more and moves CS. The phone
rings again. She drops her things once more and
answers.*)

(*Abruptly.*) What! Oh hello. Speaking. Uh huh.
Uh huh. What? Oh no. No, don't say this to me.
You can't do this to me, not now. Well, have
you got anybody else we could use? No! What
do you mean no? (*She gets cut off.*) Hello, hello.
This bloody phone! (*She puts it in her bag. It
rings again.*) Now listen, you fuckwit, you've
picked on the wrong person here. So don't you
fucking start – (*A beat.*) Sheila? Oh shit, sorry,
Sheila, I thought it was – never mind. What is
it? (*A beat.*) But it's important. Your dog's not
well. It's only a bloody dumb dog, for God's
sake. No, no I didn't mean to call your dog. Yes,
I know he's part of the family. Yes, I know you

love him more than you do your husband. It's just, well can't you give him a boneo and tell him to suck on that? (*The phone goes dead.*) Sheila! Hello, Sheila! Oh well shit you, then. (Nɪᴄᴏʟᴀ *starts to gather up her bags once more.*) I hope your fucking dog dies.

(Fʀᴀɴᴄɪs Kɪʀᴍᴀɴ *enters through the door SL.*)

FRANCIS   Come on, lad, you're gonna be late.

(Nɪᴄᴏʟᴀ *exits through the door SR as* Gᴇᴏʀɢᴇ Mᴀʀsʜᴀʟʟ Sɴʀ *enters earnestly from the wings SR.*)

Scene Three

GEORGE SNR   Francis! I'm not too late am I? He hasn't gone.

FRANCIS   No, no. He's just saying goodbye to his mother.

GEORGE SNR   Has she taken it badly?

FRANCIS   She's a woman, George.

(Cʜᴀʀʟᴇs Kɪʀᴍᴀɴ *enters through the door SL carrying a suitcase and a brown paper parcel tied with string.*)

CHARLES   Sorry, Dad. I can't leave her like that.

FRANCIS   Leave your mother to me.

GEORGE SNR   Big day, Charles. It's a proud day, Francis.

FRANCIS   It's a Monday, George.

GEORGE SNR   You're a deep one, Francis. I bet he hasn't told you how proud he is of –

FRANCIS   That's enough of that kind of talk, George.

(GEORGE JR *comes hurtling on to the stage.*)

GEORGE JNR   Charlie Farley.

CHARLES   Georgey Porgy.

                  (*They embrace.*)

GEORGE SNR   Why aren't you at work?

GEORGE JNR   They gave me a bit of time off to say goodbye
                  to our hero.

CHARLES   Hero?

GEORGE JNR   They've got bunting out in the streets and
                  across the railway station. The whole village is
                  down there waiting to see you off. I've never
                  seen anything like it. Are you coming down, Mr.
                  Kirman?

FRANCIS   We've decided it's best if we . . . No, no, we're
                  not.

GEORGE JNR   I wish I was coming with you, Charlie.

GEORGE SNR   Yes, well you're not, you're far too young.

GEORGE JNR   I'm not, I'm ready. I could do it. Those Germans
                  wouldn't know what had hit them. Bang, bang,
                  bang.

GEORGE SNR   Are you arguing with me, lad? (*A beat.* GEORGE
                  JNR *is physically deflated.*)

GEORGE JNR   No, Dad.

GEORGE SNR   Are you too young to join the army? (*Pause.*)
                  Are you?

GEORGE JNR   Yes, Dad.

CHARLES   Don't forget to call in on Dora. Make sure she's alright and get her anything she needs, do you hear me?

GEORGE JNR   (*A little hesitant.*) Eh, oh right. Yes. Yes, I can do that.

GEORGE SNR   Good luck, Charles. It's a grand thing you're doing. I'm very proud of you and *I'm* not afraid to say it.

               (*He proffers his hand and they shake*).

CHARLES   Thanks, Mr. Marshall.

GEORGE JNR   Bye, Charlie.

CHARLES   Bye, Georgey.

               (GEORGE JNR *embraces* CHARLES, *who returns the compliment.*)

GEORGE SNR   (*Starts to exit.*) George! Francis. (*Raising his voice.*) George!

GEORGE JNR   (*Calling back as he exits.*) Kill a German for me.

               (GEORGE SNR *clips* GEORGE JNR *across the head.*)

               Ow!

               (*They exit.*)

CHARLES   Are you sure me mam'll be alright?

FRANCIS   Don't worry, she'll be fine. (*Pause.*) Is Dora not popping over to see you off?

CHARLES   No. She got the morning off work when we got married. She didn't think it was right to ask for any more time.

FRANCIS	Right. Have you got everything?
CHARLES	I haven't got room for anything. Have you seen this baking? She does know I'm married, doesn't she.
FRANCIS	You've got a lot to learn, lad. Nothing comes between a mother and her boy. Not even marriage. As far as your mother's concerned, Dora has just borrowed you for a while.
CHARLES	Right. (*A beat.*) Well dad, I suppose that's it, then. (*Pause.*) I'll best be off.
FRANCIS	Aye.
CHARLES	Right then.
FRANCIS	Right, take care of yourself.
	(*It's a bit awkward. They have an inclination to cuddle.* CHARLES *moves to cuddle his dad.* FRANCIS *tenses.* FRANCIS *proffers a hand.*)
CHARLES	Bye, Dad.
	(CHARLES *pauses a moment and then shakes it.*)
FRANCIS	Bye, lad.
	(*They break hands.*)
CHARLES	Right, I'll get going then.
FRANCIS	Aye.
	(*Pause.*)
CHARLES	I'm going then.
FRANCIS	Right (*Pause.*) Well bugger off then.

CHARLES   (*He smiles.*) Yeah. (*A beat.*) Bye, Dad.

                   (CHARLES *hesitates a moment before stealing
                   himself away. He checks, turns back and looks
                   at his dad.* FRANCIS *nods approval.* NICOLA PIKE
                   *enters through the SR door, talking on the
                   phone.*)

NICOLA   Yes, Nicola Pike, that's right. I've booked –

                   (CHARLES *turns and exits quickly.* NICOLA *shivers
                   as he walks behind her. She looks at him,
                   confused, as he exits.*)

                   (*Back to the phone.*) Oh sorry, I think
                   someone's just walked over my grave.

                            Scene Four

Community Centre.

FRANCIS *stands some time watching* CHARLES *go. He exhales, turns
and makes his way off as* NICOLA *fetches the small table from US.*

NICOLA   Yes, chicken. Yes. For sixty. Oh that's great.
                   Saturday morning. Yeah, I'll be here. About ten.
                   Brill. Cheers. See you then.

                   (NICOLA *ferries the small table and two chairs
                   DSL.* MAURICE – *president of the local theatre
                   group, a larger-than-life character in his late
                   forties –bursts into the room through the SL
                   door and sings.*)

MAURICE   (*He sings.*)
                   *We're gonna hang out the washing on the
                       Siegfried Line.*
                   Have you any dirty washing, mother dear?
                   Ooocha Ooocha.

(*Spoken.*) I thought I could maybe sing a few songs from the war, for this thing of yours. You know, create the right mood.

NICOLA   I don't think that would work, Maurice.

MAURICE   Why not?

NICOLA   Cos you're shit.

MAURICE   Right, I'll ask Moira.

NICOLA   (NICOLA *stops dead in her tracks.*) Don't you dare!

MAURICE   Still not forgiven you, then.

NICOLA   It wasn't my fault.

MAURICE   That's what you say.

NICOLA   You know what the *Echo's* like. I told them it was her idea.

MAURICE   One song.

NICOLA   Don't you start winding me up. Not today. The turn has just pulled out of Saturday.

              (NICOLA *moves the trestle table from US more CS.*)

MAURICE   (*Excitedly.*) I've been having singing lessons.

NICOLA   No!

MAURICE   I could do a little spot. Oh, come on. Why not?

NICOLA   I'll tell you why not. According to the Fulstow fire safety certificate we can empty a full house from this building in under three minutes. When you sang "The Elusive Butterfly of Love" at the karaoke night, you proved it.

MAURICE	I had a sore throat. I've got new songs. I've been having lessons.
NICOLA	(*Emphatically.*) No!
MAURICE	(*Ad libs the intro to "Let Me Entertain You" by Robbie Williams.*)
NICOLA	Maurice!

(NICOLA *exits through the door SR, leaving it open.*)

NICOLA	(*Off.*) Maurice!

(NICOLA *re-enters, carrying a file of papers.* MAURICE *sings to her.*)

MAURICE	(*Singing.*) *There's nothing left for you to fear.* *Show your arse, come over here,* *Now scream.*
NICOLA	(*Shouting.*) Maurice! What is your problem?! You're not singing and that's the end of it. And how long do we have to put up with these sandbags?
MAURICE	The scouts are using them.
NICOLA	Don't you blame the bloody scouts.
MAURICE	Yeah, well the drama group might be using them as well.
NICOLA	It's your bloody drama group. So you'd better get rid of 'em, they're starting to smell and there's sand from here to hell and back.

(TIM *enters though the door SL carrying a large cardboard box.* MAURICE *starts busying himself*

*sweeping up the loose sand near the sandbags
SR.)*

NICOLA   Oh Tim, you little saviour. Is everything there?

TIM   No, I've forgotten half of it.

              (NICOLA *playfully slaps* TIM. MAURICE *breaks out
              into song.)*

MAURICE   (*Singing.*)
              *Look me up in the yellow pages
              I will be your rock of –*

NICOLA   Maurice! Can you get this box and put it into
              the concert room?

MAURICE   Not with my back, I can't.

NICOLA   Right, well go get some water.

              (MAURICE *exits through the door SR.)*

              Sorry, Tim, just put it down there and *I'll* sort
              it. And you're going to deliver the meals for me
              tomorrow lunchtime, aren't you?

              (TIM *places the box on the table DSL.)*

TIM   As long as I can leave at twelve sharp.

NICOLA   They'll be ready, promise. I'm cooking them in
              the morning.

TIM   They got beat three-nil, by the way.

NICOLA   Oh shit. I forgot. Oh bloody hell.

TIM   It's all right, I covered for you. I said you'd
              make it up to him on Saturday morning.

              (NICOLA *looks vacantly.)*

His big cup game. You'd forgotten, hadn't you.

NICOLA   (*Bluffing.*) No.

TIM   Are you gonna be late tonight?

NICOLA   No, I'll be straight home after this.

              (MAURICE *re-enters through the door SR.*)

TIM   Right, I'll see you later.

              (*They kiss and part.* TIM *goes to exit.*)

              Are you singing at this do, Maurice?

MAURICE   You see, Tim wants me to sing.

NICOLA   OUT!

              (*She flings a toilet roll at* TIM, *who ducks. It
              hits* GRAHAM, *who has just opened the door
              SL, smack on the head.* TIM *runs out laughing.*
              GRAHAM, *a curmudgeonly man in his early fifties,
              stands annoyed. He is carrying a footstool.*)

              Sorry, Graham.

GRAHAM   I've had the worst week of my life. (*A beat.*)
              And I've had some shit weeks, believe you me.

NICOLA   Oh God!

GRAHAM   I'm bunged up.

NICOLA   Evening, Graham.

GRAHAM   I've never been to the toilet for a week.

MAURICE   You should go to the doctor's; that's dangerous,
              that is.

GRAHAM   It's him that caused it; changing me tablets. I've
                  never been well since I started going to him.
                  And its not helping my piles this I'll tell you. I
                  nearly burst a bloody blood vessel last night.

NICOLA   Graham!

                  (NICOLA *carries the box off through the door SR.*)

GRAHAM   I thought me head was gonna pop off.

MAURICE   Have you tried laxatives?

GRAHAM   Laxatives! Oh no, I never thought of that.
                  'Course I bloody tried laxatives; I've got
                  Senokots coming out me arse. There isn't a
                  vindaloo within twenty miles I haven't had.

                  (NICOLA *re-enters.*)

NICOLA   Did you ask Doreen to do the table decorations
                  on Saturday?

GRAHAM   Well, the thing is . . .

MAURICE   He's scared of her.

GRAHAM   I am not scared of her.

MAURICE   I'd be scared of her. She could scare a police
                  horse.

GRAHAM   That's my wife. And I am not scared of her.

NICOLA   *I'll* ask her. What is your problem? And what's
                  that? (*Indicating footstool.*)

GRAHAM   I can't sit on those, they're too hard. This is
                  softer.

NICOLA   Well why didn't you bring a cushion?

GRAHAM   (*He hesitates.*) Doreen wouldn't let me.

MAURICE   (*A beat.*) You little shithouse.

GRAHAM   Our cushions are new.

                 (GRAHAM *hangs his coat up on the USL door.*)

MAURICE   Speaking of scary women, I bumped into Moira
                 this afternoon.

NICOLA   Don't tell me *she's* not coming.

MAURICE   Worse.

GRAHAM   She *is* coming.

MAURICE   She's baked a cake. I was never off the toilet
                 last time she baked a cake.

GRAHAM   (*Suddenly interested.*) Really?

MAURICE   Oh yeah, that lemon drizzle cake drizzled
                 alright, straight out –

NICOLA   Maurice!

MAURICE   Well at least she's not making the chocolate
                 cake for the fundraiser.

NICOLA   What?

MAURICE   I asked somebody else.

                 (NICOLA *and* GRAHAM *are stunned. They both
                 freeze and snap a look to* MAURICE.)

NICOLA   What?

MAURICE   What?

GRAHAM   (*With real shock.*) You – asked – somebody –
                 else?

NICOLA   Shit.

GRAHAM	Does Moira know?
MAURICE	No, not yet.
NICOLA	Shit.
GRAHAM	Uh hoh!

(MOIRA *enters hurriedly.* MOIRA, *a schoolteacher in her early forties, who feels a cut above the rest. She is carrying a cake in a cake box.*)

MOIRA	Sorry I'm late.
GRAHAM	Maurice has something to tell you, haven't you, Maurice.

(MAURICE *and* NICOLA *snap a fierce look to* GRAHAM, *who chuckles contentedly.* MOIRA *places the cake box on the SL end of the trestle table, hangs her coat up on the door SL and retrieves a knife from the sideboard US.*)

MAURICE	Oh, nowt much really. I know how busy you are. And I thought I would make things a little easier for you.
MOIRA	What are you blathering on about?
MAURICE	I've asked somebody else to make the chocolate cake on Saturday.

(MOIRA, *physically shocked, staggers on her feet and grabs hold of a chair to steady herself.* NICOLA *dives into her file and starts pulling sheets out at random.* GRAHAM *puts the footstool down and sits on it. His head is barely above the table.*)

GRAHAM	Oh, for God's sake.

MOIRA	(*She waves the knife around.*) But I always bake the chocolate cake. I've won awards for my chocolate cake.
MAURICE	I just thought . . .
MOIRA	People come from far and wide to look at my delicate sponge.
	(*She flails the knife around, just missing* GRAHAM, *who nearly falls off his stool.*)
GRAHAM	Well there ya go.
MAURICE	Just thought it would ease the pressure.
MOIRA	Pressure? I thrive on pressure, I'm a teacher. I suppose you put him up to this?
	(*She points the knife at* NICOLA *and again* GRAHAM *does his best to avoid the flailing knife.*)
NICOLA	Hey, I knew nothing about it. Don't blame me.
MOIRA	Who is making it?
MAURICE	Irene Mablethorpe said she would –
MOIRA	Irene Mablethorpe!
MAURICE	Well she offered and I –
MOIRA	Irene bloody Mabelthorpe.
MAURICE	And I was worried that you were doing too much.
MOIRA	She's a menace to society, is Irene Mablethorpe.
NICOLA	Can we all sit down and make a start?
MOIRA	And why she doesn't have a shave I'll never know.

MAURICE   We can have two cakes.

                   (MOIRA *retrieves plates from the sideboard
                   before furiously starting to cut the cake and
                   plate it up.*)

NICOLA   Look, let's make a start, shall we?

MOIRA   Wait until you taste this lemon drizzle. It'll
                   bring tears to your eyes.

MAURICE   (*Aside.*) You can say that again.

MOIRA   I mean, why she doesn't wear a bra is a mystery
                   to me.

NICOLA   Right, before I get on –

MOIRA   Bloody things swinging round her knees.

GRAHAM   Could I get two pieces, please?

MOIRA   Graham, what are you doing down there?

MAURICE   He's got a sore arse.

MOIRA   We are not all football hooligans, Maurice.

NICOLA   Can we all please sit down? Give me strength.
                   Right, before I get on to the topic of the roof
                   and the Fancy Dress Fundraiser on Saturday,
                   I've got something important I want to discuss.

MOIRA   Piece for you. (*She places a plate of cake in
                   front of* NICOLA.)

NICOLA   I went into the pub, I don't know, about a
                   month ago.

MOIRA   TWO pieces for you. (*She places a plate of cake
                   in front of* GRAHAM.)

NICOLA   And there was no one in.

MOIRA   (*She slams a plate down in front of* MAURICE.)
And one for you. And I hope you bloody choke
on it.

NICOLA   Moira, for God's sake! Right, as I was saying,
I went into the pub. And there was no one in,
apart from this old guy. (*An* OLD MAN *enters
from the wings SL and sits at the table DSL.*)
Sally was out the back. He was watching the
memorial service on the telly.

* * * * * * *

(NICOLA *moves into the pub and talks to the* OLD
MAN.)

NICOLA   Morning.

(*Silence.*)

Were you in the war?

(*He doesn't comment. A pause.*)

(*A little louder.*) Were you in the war?

OLD MAN   Guess how old I am?

NICOLA   Are you from round these parts?

OLD MAN   Eighty-two.

NICOLA   Oh God.

OLD MAN   I used to live round here.

NICOLA   Oh really, whereabouts?

OLD MAN   Fulstow hasn't got a war memorial, you know.

NICOLA   We must have.

OLD MAN   Oh, they talked about it. After the First World
               War they talked about it. But they didn't, on
               account of one of them being shot.

NICOLA   Isn't that the point of them?

OLD MAN   You see, one of the lads was shot as a deserter
               and someone objected to his name being
               included on the memorial. Well this got the
               wind up some of the parents who had lost lads.
               They didn't like it. They said, "There were ten
               lads born in Fulstow, ten lads played in the
               fields of Fulstow, ten lads went to school in
               Fulstow and ten lads went off to war; if there
               aren't ten names on that memorial then you
               don't include our boy's name". And they've
               never had one.

                              *   *   *   *   *   *   *

               (As NICOLA speaks, she moves out of the pub
               towards the trestle table. The OLD MAN exits
               into the wings SL.)

NICOLA   And then I turned round to speak to Sally and
               this guy disappeared. Poof. Like he wasn't there.

GRAHAM   Did they know he was a deserter?

NICOLA   Apparently.

MOIRA   I find that hard to believe.

MAURICE   You wouldn't want your son's name next to
               some coward who'd ran away.

GRAHAM   It doesn't make sense.

MOIRA   Well for once I'm inclined to agree with Ant
               and Dec.

MAUR. / GRAH. Oooooh.

MOIRA	Oh, grow up.

(MAURICE *and* GRAHAM *share a knowing look*.)

GRAHAM	Who was he, this man?
NICOLA	I don't know. Sally said that there had been no one in all morning; that I was the first customer of the day.
GRAHAM	How many had you had?
NICOLA	I hadn't had any.
GRAHAM	She'll have been drinking.
NICOLA	It was eleven o'clock in the morning.

(GRAHAM *gives a knowing look to* MAURICE *and* MOIRA *and mimes having a drink*.)

NICOLA	I hadn't been drinking. I mean, you know what Sally's like; she doesn't know what day it is half the time. She could have been wrong. The only thing was, I could have sworn he was drinking, but there was no glass.
MOIRA	Irene bloody Mablethorpe. I could spit.
NICOLA	Look, I'll cut to the chase; I want to erect a memorial with all the boys' names on it.
GRAHAM	Including the coward's?
NICOLA	Deserter, Maurice, deserter.
MAURICE	Is there a difference?
MOIRA	Oh, I don't think so. No, no, no, no. I mean I've got nothing against a memorial *per se*, but it will not include the name of a deserter. As far

	as I'm concerned a memorial is for heroes, not for cowards who ran away.
MAURICE	Hear, hear. My Uncle Wilfred was in the war.
NICOLA	Yeah, but I've been looking into it. He was shot at dawn on 23rd September 1917.
GRAHAM	Who by?
MAURICE	I'd've shot him myself, the bloody coward.
NICOLA	Well apparently it could have been members of his platoon or another platoon.
MAURICE	I hate cowards.
GRAHAM	So it *could* have been his mates.
NICOLA	Yes, if they were under orders. I've been doing a bit of research, and I think he was ill.
MAURICE	He'd have been ill if I'd got my bloody hands on him.
	(NICOLA *flicks through her pieces of paper, searching for her research. The fire alarm goes off. There is a general groan from the group, and they chunter as they start to make their way outside through the SL door.*)
GRAHAM	It's a test. Leave everything and congregate at the assembly point. Leave all your possessions. Make your way outside, please.
NICOLA	Why are we having a test now?
GRAHAM	There's never a good time for a test. Malcolm has a job to do.
NICOLA	You could have warned us.
GRAHAM	But then it wouldn't be a test, would it?

(GRAHAM *grabs an extra bit of cake. As he exits,*
CHARLES *enters, walking from the wings SR.*
GEORGE JNR *enters in hot pursuit.*)

* * * * * * *

GEORGE JNR   (*Calling after* CHARLES.) Charlie! Charlie! Wait up.

CHARLES   George. What's is it?

GEORGE JNR   I've done it, Charlie.

CHARLES   Done what?

GEORGE JNR   I've joined up.

CHARLES   What are you talking about?

GEORGE JNR   I've joined up. I've done it. I'm going to fight.

CHARLES   (*Confused.*) What? We've just talked about this.
                You're not eighteen.

GEORGE JNR   I know. But the recruiting sergeant told me to
                have a little walk round the block and come
                back when I was eighteen. So I did.

CHARLES   (*Shocked.*) And they let you join?

GEORGE JNR   Yeah.

CHARLES   You can't do this, Georgey.

GEORGE JNR   I've already done it.

CHARLES   But your dad.

GEORGE JNR   I haven't told him. You heard him. He won't
                like it. He'll be upset, I know he will. You know
                what he's like. He thinks I'm still a kid. He talks
                down to me like I'm a kid.

CHARLES   You are a kid!

GEORGE JNR   Not anymore, I'm not.

CHARLES   Listen, George, I want you to do me a favour.
                    You will do as I ask, won't you, George.

GEORGE JNR   Course I will, Charlie.

CHARLES   This is important. I want you to go and tell the
                    recruiting board the truth about how old you
                    are. I want you to forget all this nonsense about
                    going to fight.

GEORGE JNR   I don't wanna miss out on all the fun.

CHARLES   Fun!

GEORGE JNR   Yes! Cos it'll be all over very soon. That's what
                    everyone's saying. Christmas, apparently. And I
                    wanna be a hero like you.

CHARLES   You keep saying this. My medals were for good
                    conduct. Look, war isn't fun. Georgey. You're
                    a great, courageous mate. But as a friend, I beg
                    you, go and tell the truth and stay here and look
                    after Dora, like you promised. The village needs
                    fit young men, like you.

GEORGE JNR   So does the war effort.

CHARLES   Look, if you won't tell them, then I will. You
                    can't do this. I'm sorry, Georgey, but I'm gonna
                    tell your dad.

                    (CHARLES *walks back towards Fulstow.* GEORGE JNR
                    intercepts him.)

GEORGE JNR   No, Charlie! You can't, you'll miss your train.
                    (*With real sincerity.*) I'm ready. I am, honest. I'm
                    not a kid anymore. I've grown up. I'm stronger
                    than most people ten years older than me.
                    I'm doing a man's job. I'm old enough to get
                    married. So why can't I fight? . . . I've thought it

through. Believe me, Charlie, I know what I'm
doing, and I'm all right. Honest.

(*He plants a big kiss on* CHARLES' *cheek.*)

Be happy for me, Charlie.

(GEORGE JNR *goes to exit.* CHARLES *watches
him.* GEORGE JNR *turns and smiles at* CHARLES
as NICOLA, MAURICE, GRAHAM *and* MOIRA *enter
through the SL door.* GEORGE JNR *exits through
the SR wing. The fire alarm goes off again,
briefly forcing* NICOLA *and* GRAHAM *to stop. The
fire alarm stops. They breathe a sigh of relief.*
CHARLES *exits through the SL wing.* MOIRA *sits SL
of the trestle table.*)

* * * * * * *

GRAHAM   (*Sitting on radiator SL.*) It's colder in here than it
                is out there, and it's Baltic out there.

                (*The fire alarm goes off again.*)

NICOLA   (*Shouting.*) Malcolm! (*The alarm stops.*) I swear
                I'm gonna bloody swing for him. Look, let's
                get back down to what we were talking about.
                (*Waving a piece of paper in the air and taking
                position SR of the trestle table.*) Right when the
                war broke out, he was one of the first lot over
                there.

                (MAURICE *enters through the SL door, wiping his
                hands on his trousers.*)

                Where've you been?

MAURICE   (*Making his way and sitting at the DSL table.*)
                Sorry.

NICOLA   And within ten days of going out – ten days,
                mind you – he fought in the Battle of Mons and,

I'm telling you, there were heavy casualties.
Some caused by our own men.

GRAHAM   (*Now sitting US at the trestle table on his
                footstool.*) What you talking about?

NICOLA   Well, when they were returning to the trenches
                they thought they were Germans and started
                firing at them. They were in no man's land,
                being shot at from both sides.

MAURICE   I don't believe that.

NICOLA   It's bloody true. I'm telling you, it's true. And
                five weeks later he was in the battle of La
                Bassee where he got injured, for the first time,
                and was sent home. When he returned to
                France he went straight into another bloody
                cock-up known as the Battle of Auburs Ridge.

MAURICE   I've seen the film.

NICOLA   Have you?

MAURICE   Yeah. The Battle of Auburs Ridge. It was a
                cowboy film.

GRAHAM   John Wayne was in it.

NICOLA   It's not a cowboy film.

MAURICE   I think he was.

GRAHAM   And Glenn Ford was the sheriff.

NICOLA   It wasn't a bloody cowboy film. It's a place in
                France. For God's sake.

MAURICE   (*Mouthing to* GRAHAM *as* NICOLA *consults her
                papers.*) I saw it.

NICOLA   Now listen, there were eleven thousand British
                casualties in one day.

MAURICE	That's a Friday night in Hull.
NICOLA	(*To Maurice.*) I don't know why I'm bothering with this. I'm running out of patience with you.
GRAHAM	Sounds like a blood bath.
MAURICE	Yeah, like a Friday night in –
NICOLA	Right! Either you take it seriously or go.
MAURICE	I'm sorry, Nicola, but we know that there were heavy casualties in the First World War. Everyone knows that.
NICOLA	But it doesn't make it right. Listen to this. (NICOLA *searches through her papers.*)
MOIRA	Anybody like any more cake?
GRAHAM	I'll have a piece, please, Moira. It's nearly as nice as your chocolate cake.
MOIRA	Sorry, I didn't hear you, Graham.
GRAHAM	I said (*And he speaks up a bit.*) it's nearly as nice as your chocolate cake.
MOIRA	I thought that's what you said.
	(MOIRA *cuts* GRAHAM *a piece of cake and starts to tidy up.* NICOLA *produces a fresh sheet of paper.*)
NICOLA	Got it.
MOIRA	Anybody else for cake?
NICOLA	Are you listening to this?
	(*As there are no takers,* MOIRA *starts to clear away.*)

He was in the battle of the Somme. There were
sixty thousand casualties, and nearly twenty
thousand killed – on the first day. Charles'
battalion went over the top at seven thirty,
and by nine o'clock almost half of them were
injured, including Kirman. Twenty thousand
killed on the first day!

MOIRA   Yeah, but surely the court will have known this.
They will have taken it into account when they
sentenced him. (*Pause.*) Wouldn't they?

NICOLA   But the point is that shell shock wasn't
recognised then, like it is now.

MOIRA   Look, we can't start applying our standards on
theirs. There were also murderers and other
people shot. Wasn't there?

NICOLA   (*Hesitates.*) Well, yes.

MOIRA   Exactly. It's like saying that people shouldn't
have been sent to Australia for stealing a loaf
of bread, but they were. Those were the rules
then, the rules of the day, and people had to
abide by them or face the consequences of
their actions. When he deserted, he knew what
could happen.

NICOLA   He was terrified!

MOIRA   And so were thousands of others. Scared half to
death, I don't doubt, but they didn't desert.

NICOLA   You're missing the point; he was ill, medically
ill, but you don't know what that's like or, more
importantly, you just don't want to know.

MOIRA   Don't I?

NICOLA   No, you don't. It's because it wasn't your idea,
isn't it?

MOIRA   Well it doesn't matter whose idea it is; you'll
             take the credit for it.

NICOLA   I told the *Echo* the Vintage Tractor Rally was
             your idea.

MOIRA   Huh!

NICOLA   The only reason you're still annoyed about
             that is that it's *you* that's bothered about
             appearance. You don't wanna know about
             these people. You don't care what they've been
             through.

MOIRA   Don't I? Well let me tell you something; my
             father was in the war. That's shut you up, hasn't
             it? And he won medals. But let me tell you this,
             Nicola Pike, it wasn't easy. He was never the
             same man when he came out as when he went
             in. But he wouldn't talk about it. My mother
             had a terrible time with him. We all did. So
             don't you talk to me about understanding what
             went on, about caring. But he did his duty.
             And if you think I am going to have the name
             of some deserter sitting alongside honest-to-
             goodness soldiers like my father, well you've got
             another thing coming. So don't start patronising
             me with your little do-goody crusade, cos it
             doesn't wash.

GRAHAM   And he *was* tried before a court of law and
             found guilty.

NICOLA   But the trials were flawed.

MOIRA   What, all of them?

NICOLA   It was that bastard Haig who kept authorising
             them.

MOIRA   General Haig received a state funeral.

NICOLA   He was a butcher.

MOIRA   From what I remember of my private education,
              General Haig had thousands of requests for
              people being shot at dawn and he turned down
              ninety percent of them. Didn't he? (*A pause.*)
              Didn't he?

NICOLA   I don't know.

MOIRA   You don't know. She doesn't know. Well I think
              you should get your facts straight before you
              come charging in here with your half-baked
              ideas. I think we have wasted enough time on
              this already. Let's vote.

NICOLA   We haven't got quorum.

MOIRA   And we very rarely have it, so don't start that
              one. All those in favour of a war memorial
              to commemorate those who died in the war
              including Charles Kirman's name, raise your
              hands.

              (NICOLA *shoots her hand into the air. Pause.*)

NICOLA   Graham, for God's sake.

MOIRA   Leave him alone.

GRAHAM   Hey, I can stick up for meself.

              (*Pause. They all turn and look at his little head
              peering above the table.*)

MAURICE   (*Patting him on the head.*) You tell them, big
              fella.

MOIRA   Those against?

              (MOIRA *and* MAURICE *raise their hands.* GRAHAM
              hesitates.)

GRAHAM	He was found guilty. (*He raises his hand.*)
MOIRA	Right, that's settled. The motion has been defeated.
MAURICE	But we should still build one.
GRAHAM	Yeah, definitely.
NICOLA	Not without his name on, you can't.
MOIRA	And why can't we?
NICOLA	Because I won't allow it; it was my idea –
MOIRA	And it's a good one, and one I think we should embrace.
MAURICE	So do I.
NICOLA	You bastards. Well that's it; you'll get no help from me. And then we'll see how far you get. Here, sort the bloody lot out yourself. (*She throws a file across the table.*)
MOIRA	That's just typical, isn't it.
NICOLA	Without me organising every damm thing this committee would fall apart.
MOIRA	Maybe if you didn't interfere as much with things that don't concern you, this committee might just run a bit smoother. It's because of you that nobody bothers to turn up.
NICOLA	Who the hell are you talking to?
MOIRA	This happens every time she doesn't get her own way.
NICOLA	You jumped-up little shit.

MOIRA	Oh, here she goes again. You've got no class, have you?
NICOLA	Class. I'll show you class in a minute, you snobby little cow.
MAURICE	(*Trying to lighten the situation.*) Would anybody like a cup of tea?
MOIRA	(*Aghast.*) Right! I'm not putting up with this anymore. You can't reason with this. I think we should have a short break so that some people can leave.
	(MOIRA *exits through the SL door.*)
NICOLA	(*Calling after her.*) And your chocolate cake's the shits.
GRAHAM	Nicola! For God's sake, calm down.
NICOLA	Calm down. Calm down. Did you hear what she called me? She said I've got no class. I've a good mind to knock her fucking head off.
MAURICE	Oh, cos that's real classy.
NICOLA	(*Aggressively.*) What?
MAURICE	Shall we have a cup of tea?
GRAHAM	You can't go round shouting at people like that.
NICOLA	She puts the spoke in everything I try and do. She's bloody jealous, that's her problem. Jealous as the day is long. Well, I've put up with it for too long. No, I'm finished with her and I'm finished with you lot.
GRAHAM	What have we done?
NICOLA	You sided with her.

GRAHAM   All we did was vote.

NICOLA   You're bloody spineless, the lot of you. Well,
              you can stick your roof, stick your fundraiser and
              stick your committee up your arse. But I'll tell
              you this for nowt: there is no memorial going up
              in Fulstow unless it has ten names on it.

MAURICE   That's not up to you.

              (NICOLA *moves towards him aggressively and
              scared,* MAURICE *takes flight.*)

              Oooh me back.

              (NICOLA *thinks better of attacking him and exits
              through the door SR to retrieve her belongings.*)

GRAHAM   (*Calling after her.*) Nicola.

              (*Silence.*)

              We've got to stop her.

MAURICE   Stop her! She nearly bloody attacked me.

GRAHAM   That lass wouldn't hurt you.

MAURICE   That's not a lass. It's Nicola Pike! The last time
              she stormed out of a meeting, she hit Peter over
              the head with an exit sign.

GRAHAM   Look, we are right in the bloody shit now.

MAURICE   We can sort this out.

GRAHAM   How? The roof needs repairing, we can't get
              money out of the bank.

MAURICE   Why not?

GRAHAM   Cos we have to wait till the treasurer comes
              back from his round-the-world cruise.

MAURICE   How can he afford that?

                 (GRAHAM *glares at him, amazed at his stupidity.*)

GRAHAM   We've got this Fancy Dress Fundraiser
                 thingymebob on Saturday – and I hate fancy
                 dress. So now Moira presumably is going to
                 take charge – and we all know what a disaster
                 she is – of a committee that is so depleted
                 there appears to only be you and me who can
                 be bothered to turn up. Without Nicola this
                 whole bloody committee will collapse. It'll be a
                 disaster. We have to stop her. Get her to change
                 her mind.

                 (GRAHAM *freezes. He is obviously in serious
                 discomfort.*)

                 Oh my God.

MAURICE   What?

GRAHAM   Oh hell.

MAURICE   What?

GRAHAM   I can't move

MAURICE   You can't move.

GRAHAM   I can't fucking move.

MAURICE   What do you mean, you can't move?

GRAHAM   I mean I can't move.

MAURICE   Shall I get someone? Shall I get Nicola?

GRAHAM   I've shit meself.

MAURICE   What?

GRAHAM   I have. I've done it. I've shit meself . . .

(MAURICE *guffaws with laughter.*)

It's not bloody funny. I'll have to get home. I need the toilet, I need it quick.

(GRAHAM *waddles across the room.*)

MAURICE   I'll get the door.

GRAHAM   You've got to stop Nicola.

MAURICE   Me?

GRAHAM   Well who else is gonna stop her? You've got to stop her. Aaargh, it's running down me bloody leg.

MAURICE   Graham! You've forgotten your soft stool.

(*As* GRAHAM *waddles past* MAURICE *to exit through the door SL,* MAURICE *slaps his backside.*)

GRAHAM   Aaaah, you bastard.

(DORA *enters from the wings SL, humming and singing 'Lily of Laguna' to the baby she cradles in her arms.* MAURICE, *in sheer panic, runs back and forward between* NICOLA's *exit door and* GRAHAM's *not knowing whether to confront* NICOLA *or make a break for it. He decides to go for* NICOLA *and exits through the door SR.*)

Scene Five

December 1916. CHARLES *enters through the door SR in full military uniform and stands watching* DORA *and the baby, admiringly. He has lost some of his sparkle and is not the confident, bright young man of earlier.*

CHARLES   Hello, Dora (*He removes his cap.*)

DORA

Charlie? (*A beat.*) Oh God! Why didn't you write? Why didn't you tell me you were coming home? (*She struggles to stand with the baby in hand and with the other she touches up her hair.*) Look at me. You should have let me know.

CHARLES

I th . . . thought you liked surprises.

DORA

I do.

(DORA *looks down at the baby and then up at* CHARLES. *She smiles.*)

Look, darling, this is your daddy. I've told you all about him, haven't I? Yes I have. Well he's here. He is. He's come to see his little girl. Yes he has. (*She looks up to* CHARLES.) Say hello to your daughter, Charlie.

(CHARLES *walks slowly forward, hesitates and enthralled looks at the baby.*)

Don't you want to hold her?

(CHARLES *backs away.*)

She won't bite.

(CHARLES, *his hand shaking, approaches the baby and gently touches her head. He recoils quickly.*)

What is it, Charlie?

(*She hands the baby over and* CHARLES *shakes as he tentatively takes hold of her.* DORA *watches* CHARLES' *fascination with the baby.*)

I hope you don't mind, but I've called her Dora. (CHARLES *looks at* DORA.) After her mother. (CHARLES *moves quickly to the table DSL.*)

Oh, Charlie.

Scene Six

NICOLA *comes bursting into the room through the door SR, hotly followed by* MAURICE. *She gathers up the papers and her file from the table.* DORA *takes the baby from* CHARLES. CHARLES *removes his coat and sits, troubled, at the small table DSL.*

MAURICE   Nicola, let's just sit down and talk about this?

NICOLA   You can't talk to her. You can't reason with the unreasonable. She won't listen, everything has to be on her terms.

MAURICE   That's why I asked Irene Mablethorpe to make the chocolate cake.

NICOLA   You know, Maurice, that was a good move. Dangerous, but good. Class! I'll show her class.

MAURICE   You see, me and you are on the same page.

NICOLA   Oh, bloody hell, I hope not. I'm going.

                   (*She moves to exit.*)

MAURICE   Graham shat himself.

NICOLA   He what?

MAURICE   He did. Moira's lemon drizzle cake did what a box of Senokots and six vindaloos couldn't. He's gone home with shit running down –

NICOLA   Right, I get the picture. Right, where's me coat? I'm gonna go and see Danny. That'll wipe the smile off her face.

MAURICE   Danny?

NICOLA   Right, me coat.

                   (NICOLA *exits through the door SR.*)

MAURICE   (*The penny drops.*) Oh shit. Not. Danny. You
                 can't talk to Danny.

                 (MAURICE *hightails it after her and closes the
                 door. There is a knock at the same SR door.*)

                         Scene Seven

DORA *answers it and* FRANCIS *enters. He removes his hat.*

FRANCIS   Dora.

                 (CHARLES *turns to see him. He is shocked, and
                 his demeanour changes. He stands. He is a little
                 scared.*)

DORA   Francis. (*An awkward silence.*) I was just going
                 to put the baby to bed.

                 (DORA *exits through the door SL.* FRANCIS *and*
                 CHARLES *stand a while.* FRANCIS, *upright, stares
                 straight at* CHARLES, *who avoids eye contact.*
                 CHARLES *starts to shake.*)

FRANCIS   Alright, lad?

CHARLES   Alright, Dad.

FRANCIS   Family?

CHARLES   Good.

FRANCIS   And the baby?

CHARLES   Sh-sh-she's beautiful.

                 (*Pause.*)

FRANCIS   You've never been up.

CHARLES   N, n, n, n, no I've, . . .

FRANCIS   You've never been up to see your mother.

CHARLES   I was g-g-gonna get meself straight f-f-first.

FRANCIS   Have we upset you, lad?

CHARLES   N-n-n-n-no, nowt like that.

FRANCIS   Have I done something I don't know about? (*A pause as he waits for an answer.*) Your mother's beside herself. I don't understand it, lad. I don't know what you're playing at. You've been home a week. And you've not bothered to come up and see your own mother. (*A pause.*) And you can stop all this crying nonsense. (CHARLES *looks up, horrified. A deafening silence.*) Dora told us. She told us all about it. Crying for no good reason at all hours of the day and night. You're a grown man. You need to pull yourself together, lad, and you need to do it quickly.

CHARLES   It's b-b-been d-d-d-difficult.

FRANCIS   (*He mimics him.*) It's b-b-been d-d-difficult, has it? What are you stuttering like that for? It's b-b-b-b-been d-d-difficult. Of course it's difficult; there's a war on.

CHARLES   It's the n-n-oise. The sh-sh-ells exploding in my h-h-h-h-ead all the t-t-t-ime.

FRANCIS   (*He digs him.*) I'm telling you and I'm telling you now; I don't want to see a son of mine crying in the corner like a baby. I hope the children haven't seen you. What sort of a way is that to bring up kids? Have you not got any pride? Stand up straight, lad. Right, you get up to see your mother first thing in the morning, do you hear me?

                 (DORA *enters through SL door.*)

(*Strongly.*) Do you hear me?

CHARLES   Yes, D-d-d-ad.

(FRANCIS *notices* DORA. *He walks to the door SR, turns, looks at* CHARLES *and shakes his head.*)

FRANCIS   Dora.

(*He puts on his hat and exits.* CHARLES *fights his tears.*)

DORA   I had to tell him. I had to tell someone. I don't know what to do. I want to help. I thought that once you'd been home a while that you would . . . get back to normal. Let me help. Talking about it might help.

(*A loud knock on the door SR.* CHARLES *jumps and panics.*)

Hey, it's alright. It's alright. It's only the door. Sssh. Charles, will you go and see a doctor? I know it can't be easy, but I think it might help you deal with things.

(*Another loud knock.* CHARLES *reacts.*)

(*Shouting.*) Just coming. (*Spoken.*) We need to get you some help. Promise me you will go and see a doctor?

(*Another knock.* CHARLES *reacts.*)

DORA   I'm coming. Hey, it's alright, there's nothing to worry about.

(*Another loud knock on the door.* DORA *answers the door. A* MILITARY POLICEMAN *is stood there.*)

M.P.   Charles Kirman.

CHARLES	D-D-Dora could you get my th-th-th-ings?
DORA	But Charles –
CHARLES	My th-th-things, please, D-D-Dora.

(CHARLES *exits through the SR door,* DORA *grabs* CHARLES' *cap and runs after him.*)

DORA	Charlie. Charlie.

(*As* DORA *exits leaving the door open,* NICOLA *enters through it, pursued by* MAURICE.)

Scene Eight

NICOLA *enters, wearing her coat, followed by* MAURICE.

NICOLA	He's been studying military history, at university. Bit of an expert, by all accounts.
MAURICE	It's Moira's nephew!
NICOLA	Is it?
MAURICE	Oh, you bugger.
NICOLA	What?
MAURICE	Oh no. No. No, you can't do that. It's Moira's nephew. She is going to be apoplectic.
NICOLA	Really? I never thought of that. That will be a shame.
MAURICE	Nicola, you can't do that. Just because you lost the vote. Just because she got one over on you.
NICOLA	You don't think this is over, do you?

MAURICE   I'll tell you what; just stay and *we'll* talk this
           through. We need you. The committee needs
           you.

NICOLA   Will she apologise?

MAURICE   She's a reasonable woman and I'm sure –

NICOLA   Will she apologise?

MAURICE   We'll all sit round a table and –

NICOLA   Will she apologise?

MAURICE   Most people are reasonable.

NICOLA   And I'm not.

MAURICE   I didn't say that.

NICOLA   But that's what you're implying.

MAURICE   (*Confused.*) What?

NICOLA   No, Maurice, she won't apologise and you
           know she won't. No, I'm sorry, but this is me
           and this committee through. Do you think I've
           got class?

MAURICE   (*A beat.*) Well . . .

NICOLA   What?

           (*She moves towards him and he runs away. She
           changes her mind and starts to exit.*)

MAURICE   Oh yeah, definitely.

NICOLA   (*Backing off.*) You're not worth it.

MAURICE   What if I change my vote?

NICOLA   Maurice, grow a pair.

(NICOLA *exits through the door SL.*)

MAURICE   (*He calls after her.*) Nicola.

                   (MAURICE *pauses for second, and then runs out
                   after her as* TIM, *agitated, enters from the wings
                   SR wearing a dressing gown carrying a cup of
                   tea. He makes a phone call. No answer. He sits
                   at the table DSL.*)

                   Scene Nine

NICOLA *giggles from behind the door SL. She enters. Hangs her
coat and bag on the back of the door. Switches on the light and
makes her way across the room to sit on the sandbags DSR. She
has been drinking.* TIM *speaks. He frightens the life out of* NICOLA.

TIM   It's two o'clock in the morning.

NICOLA.   Oh God. I'm sorry. I've been round Danny's.
                   Danny. You know Danny. He's a militarily
                   expert.

                   (*She giggles, sits on the sandbags and, with
                   great relief, removes her shoes and plays with
                   her feet.*)

TIM   Till two o'clock.

NICOLA   (*A realisation of* TIM's *implication.*) Is it two
                   o'clock? Look, I'm sorry. I've had a hell of a
                   night. But, I've found out some amazing stuff.
                   He didn't have anybody defend him.

TIM   You said you were coming straight home.

NICOLA   No, no, no, this is important. He went for trial –

TIM   When is it not important? Eh? The Vintage
                   Tractor Rally was important, the Christmas
                   Fundraiser was important. Delivering meals

	to old people is important. It's always bloody important.

NICOLA   Look, I'm sorry. I'll make it up to you.

TIM   The boys have joined the cadets.

NICOLA   (*A pause.*) What?

TIM   You heard.

NICOLA   Is this some kind of joke?

TIM   It's no joke. I wouldn't joke about things like that.

NICOLA   The fucking cadets!

TIM   Yes.

NICOLA   Well they can unjoin.

TIM   They wanted to join.

NICOLA   And you let them.

TIM   Yes! Yes. Yes, I let them. It's what they wanted.

NICOLA   I don't care. What have we talked about!?

TIM   All their mates are there.

NICOLA   Look, it might be alright for other boys, but not mine.

TIM   You can't say that.

NICOLA   I can. Yes, I can. I've just said it. I don't want a son of mine with a gun in his hand. What's wrong with that? Do you? Do you want to see our Piers or Toby with a gun in his hand? (*A beat.*) Do you? They train them to kill people. And once they get in there, they're brainwashed, for Queen and Country. "Up the Regiment", and all that shit.

TIM   They wanted to talk to you about it, but they can never find the right moment.

NICOLA   Don't you dare.

TIM   You're always too busy. Dashing here and there. You just seem to spend so much time doing for other people rather than us here.

NICOLA   Be careful, Tim.

TIM   But now that you've finished with this business.

Nicola   Who said I was finished?

TIM   You. You've quit.

NICOLA   I've not quit. I've resigned from that bloody cowboy committee, but I've not quit.

TIM   Oh no, Nicola.

NICOLA   Since when have I ever quit?

TIM   It was a hundred years ago. Who the hell's bothered?

NICOLA   I am. I'm bothered. And you should be. (A beat.) I know him.

TIM   You know him? Don't be so bloody stupid.

NICOLA   I do. You can mock. But I know him. I can see him. This man who was ill. This poor, poorly young man, shot by his own mates. Is there only me that can see that that's fundamentally wrong? You understand that, don't you?

TIM   (A pause.) Okay. Okay, I'll do a deal with you.

NICOLA   A deal! You want to do a deal!

TIM   You carry on with this charade until
                Remembrance Day in November, as long as you
                don't try and stop the boys going to the cadets.

Nicola   We're talking about peoples' lives and you want
                to do a deal. He was somebody's son.

TIM   And what about your sons?

Nicola   You don't get it, do you? They have a choice.

TIM   Do they?

NICOLA   Yes. They can choose. But he didn't have a
                choice. He had to go. They all did. And he was
                frightened and scared and no one helped him,
                no one listened to him, and people shot him.
                They deserted him! Well I'm not gunnoo. I'm
                gonna be there for him. It's not an either or.

TIM   Isn't it?

NICOLA   No.

TIM   We'll see.

NICOLA   What does that mean?

TIM   You carry on with this little game and we'll see
                what the consequences are

                (*He exits into the wings SR.*)

NICOLA   Are you threatening me? Don't threaten me.
                Don't you walk out on me. Come here.

                (*She exits in pursuit of him.* MOIRA, *dressed as
                The Queen, enters through the door SR.*)

Scene 10

Offstage we hear a Yorkshire Elvis Presley impersonator singing 'Burning Love.'

	(MOIRA *busies herself collecting dinner plates from the sideboard and placing them on the trestle table. She continues to count them. MAURICE, dressed as a rabbit, enters hurriedly.*)
MOIRA	Where's the rest of the plates?
MAURICE	(*In a panic, notices The Queen and curtsies hurriedly.*) I don't know. We need more chairs.
MOIRA	And Maureen, Winnie, Doris and the rest of the cooks haven't turned up.
	(GRAHAM *enters through the door SL, dressed in a tutu, walking gingerly, and with his back to audience, hangs up his coat.*)
MAURICE	What the hell are you wearing? You look ridiculous dressed like that.
GRAHAM	It was Doreen. Well I told her. I put my foot down. I told her once and for all.
	(*He turns to face the audience revealing a black eye.*)
	I'll never do that again.
	(MAURICE *laughs.*)
	She threw a Breville four-slice sandwich toaster right at me. And she knows I'm not well. I'm loose. I've never been off the toilet since that meeting. I feel as though my arse has exploded. And this tutu is doing me no favours, I can tell you that.

MOIRA   Well why are you wearing it?

MAURICE   Doreen made him.

GRAHAM   Shurrup.

MOIRA   The cooks haven't turned up.

GRAHAM   Well, have you rung them?

MOIRA   They knew when it was on.

GRAHAM   Nicola always rings them.

MOIRA   Well Nicola is not here, is she.

MAURICE   They'll go mad out there; they've paid fifteen
                 pounds a head for this little lot and the
                 Yorkshire Elvis isn't going down very well.

GRAHAM   Who booked a Yorkshire Elvis?

                 (GRAHAM *opens the SR door to look at Elvis. He
                 immediately closes it again.*)

MAURICE   He's cheap.

GRAHAM   He's shite.

MAURICE   And it was last minute.

GRAHAM   And we promised them a meal.

MOIRA   Well, can someone ring the cooks?

GRAHAM   At this time? What do you expect them to do?
                 Shit a meal?

MOIRA   Will you stop swearing? I am sick of all this bad
                 language. Have you got any better ideas?

GRAHAM   Ring Nicola.

MOIRA	We are not ringing Nicola.
MAURICE	I've already rang her.
MOIRA	What!
MAURICE	It went to answer machine.
MOIRA	She will have done that on purpose. She'll be loving this.
MAURICE	(MAURICE's *phone rings*.) It's Nicola.
GRAHAM	Well answer it.
MAURICE	Moira doesn't want me to.
MOIRA	Answer the fucking thing.
MAURICE	Hi, Nicola. We've got a problem down here. (*Pause as he listens*.) You'd love to help. She'd love to help. But you're in the Maldives. She's in the Maldives. Oh, you're only kidding. She's only kidding. Well first of all, the cooks haven't turned up. (*Pause*.) No she didn't ring them. (*A pause*.) Yes it was a stupid thing to do. (*A beat*.) Yes she is here. (*Pause*.) I don't know if she wants you to help or not. I'll ask her. Do you want her to help?
MOIRA	Yes, I want her to help.
MAURICE	Yes she does. (*Pause*.) You want to hear it from her. She wants to hear it from you.
	(*He offers the phone and* MOIRA *takes it and wipes it on her dress before she answers*.)
MOIRA	Hello. (*Pause, she braces herself*.) Yes I would like your help. Uh huh. Uh huh. Uh huh. (*Shocked*.) What? (*Pause*.) Okay. Alright then. I will. But on the condition that you accept

whatever decision is made. (*Pause.*) Tonight!
Well I don't know about tonight. Just a minute.
She'll come and help if we have another
meeting about Charles Kirman tonight after the
do has finished.

GRAHAM   Yes, bloody hell anything. There's a Yorkshire
                man out there dying on his blue suede arse.

MOIRA   (*She speaks into the phone.*) Okay, you're on.

MAURICE   (*Excited.*) Yes! (*They both look to him.*) That's
                good, isn't it!

MOIRA   Right, come on. We've got to get the ovens on.
                Let's go, come on.

                (GRAHAM *opens the door SR and* CHARLES KIRMAN
                enters. MOIRA *collects her plates and exits, with*
                MAURICE *and* GRAHAM *following. As the door
                slams shut* CHARLES KIRMAN *jumps. He makes his
                way into his cell and sits down and leans on the
                sandbags DSR.*)

                        Scene Eleven

(NICOLA *enters through the door SR with* DANNY, *who carries files,
papers and a plate with a piece of chocolate cake.* NICOLA *moves
the trestle table further DS.*)

DANNY   You told me she knew that I was coming.

NICOLA   I must have forgotten.

DANNY   Why didn't you tell her?

NICOLA   I forgot.

DANNY   You've done this on purpose.

NICOLA   What difference does it make?

DANNY   What difference does it make?! Do you know
             Aunty Moira?

NICOLA   Oh, for God's sake.

DANNY   What am I going to do?

NICOLA   Maybe you should just man up.

DANNY   Maybe I should go. I'm gonna go. I'm going.

             (*He places the chocolate cake on the table and
             makes his way to the SL door.* NICOLA *heads him
             off.*)

NICOLA   You're going! What are you talking about,
             you're going? Bloody grow up. She's only your
             bloody Aunty. She can't tell you what to do.

DANNY   She tells everyone what to do.

NICOLA   You have to stand up to her! For crying out
             loud!

DANNY   That's easy for you to say.

NICOLA   For God's sake you're an adult. Now sit down
             and . . . have a bit of chocolate cake.

             (DANNY *sits.* GRAHAM *enters through SR door and
             makes his way to the DSL table.*)

GRAHAM   Well I don't know how we got away with that,
             but we did. How did you do that at such short
             notice?

NICOLA   I just happened to have all those chickens going
             spare.

DANNY   Oh, bloody hell!

GRAHAM   You knew this was going to happen.

NICOLA	Me? No.
DANNY	She's gonna kill me.
GRAHAM	And you put Winnie and Doris up to it.
NICOLA	Now why would I do a thing like that?!

(MAURICE *bursts in through the SR door.*)

MAURICE	(*Singing.*) *I ain't nothing but a Hound Dog* *Crying all the time* *Ooocha, ooocha.*
NIC. / GRAH.	Maurice.
MAURICE	Did you know that by 2040 experts predict that a third of the world's population will be Elvis impersonators?
GRAHAM	Yes, and every one of them will be better than that thing we've had on here tonight.
MAURICE	He wasn't that bad.
GRAHAM	Not that bad. Me nana would have been better than him. And she's been dead twenty years.
DANNY	Well, I'm not gonna stand for it. She can't tell me what to do.

(MOIRA *enters through the SR door.*)

MOIRA	Right, that's it; everyone's gone. (*She retrieves a chair that is next to the radiator. She addresses* DANNY.) Right, you. I think you'd better go home.
DANNY	Right, bye everybody.

(*He makes to go.*)

NICOLA	Danny!

(DANNY *hesitates*.)

DANNY

Right. (*Plucking up the courage*.) You can't tell me what to do anymore, Aunty Moira. I'm an adult.

MOIRA

Blow your nose.

(MOIRA *makes her way and sits at the SR end of CS table*. DANNY *sits at the SL end of table*. NICOLA *sits at the USL end of the table next to* DANNY.)

MAURICE

Can't we do this tomorrow?

NICOLA

I know it's late, but this is important and I'll be quick.

GRAHAM

(*Sitting on the* DSL *table*.) Well, personally I don't think it is that important. We've gone best part of a hundred years without one, but unless we get that roof mended we're in real bother.

NICOLA

Look, if we go ahead with the memorial, *I'll* raise the money for the roof.

GRAHAM

How do we know you won't walk out again?

NICOLA

Because I give you my word.

MOIRA

Huh?

GRAHAM

Can we not have a meeting about whether we are going to have a meeting, and just get on with it?

MOIRA

Alright, a few minutes; that's all, cos I've not eaten.

MAURICE

(*Producing a carrot*.) Would you like a carrot? (*A pause*.) Please yourself.

(MAURICE *sits next to* NICOLA. GRAHAM, *extremely uncomfortable, pulls his tutu out from up his bum.*)

GRAHAM   (*He sighs.*) Now, I know why they called it *The Nutcracker.*

(GRAHAM *tries to get comfortable for most of the scene.*)

NICOLA   Yeah. Right, now listen; Charles Kirman went AWOL after he'd been injured at the Battle of the Somme. And we all know about that. But let me tell you, he went AWOL at the same time his daughter was born. Is that a coincidence or what?! After going through hell he probably thought, "I'm gonna go and see my baby while I have the chance," and who could blame him for that?

MOIRA   Look, that's all well and good but it's a fairy story. You're just joining dots to make your version of events.

DANNY   History is a version of joining dots.

MOIRA   And many people had babies they didn't see. It's unfortunate, but it's wartime. And that's what happens in wartime.

(*Although always wary of* MOIRA, DANNY *comes into his own when talking about history.*)

DANNY   (*Referring to his files.*) And then he had to wait three months for his trial; three months when he didn't know whether they were going to kill him or not. But they didn't; they gave him one year's imprisonment with hard labour. But, three weeks later they changed their mind, suspended it and sent him back to the front.

NICOLA	Can you imagine what must have been going on in his head! That would have sent anybody over the edge.
DANNY	And in Capital Cases he will have been faced with a jury of three high-ranking officers.
NICOLA	And he had no one defending him.
MAURICE	He must have!
NICOLA	No, he didn't.
DANNY	He *could* have had someone.
MAURICE	I bet he did.
NICOLA	He didn't. And the prosecution had a field day, calling and cross-examining people. But Charles didn't.
MAURICE	I bet he did.
NICOLA	Maurice. He bloody didn't. His life was at stake, and he didn't defend himself. He just stood there not speaking.
MOIRA	Because he knew he was guilty!
NICOLA	Because he was scared shitless.
DANNY	And once the verdict was reached they couldn't pass sentence until the commanding officer had his say. He basically had to say two things: one, whether he had the makings of a good soldier or, two, if he thought the accused's execution would be good for discipline.
GRAHAM	'Ang on, you're saying people were shot to . . . bring the other troops into line, to stop them from misbehaving or deserting or whatever?

NICOLA   Yeah, I know. It's pathetic isn't it!

GRAHAM   That's unbelievable.

NICOLA   I know, but it happened.

MAURICE   What did Charles' commanding officer say?

DANNY   Nothing.

GRAHAM   And Charles didn't say anything at all.

MAURICE   I bet he did.

NICOLA   He did make a couple of statements, on oath.

MAURICE   Told ya.

NICOLA   He said.

              (*A spot on* CHARLES KIRMAN, *who stands DSR.*)

                          *   *   *   *   *   *   *

CHARLES   I have been out abroad in India seven years and
              four months. I often suffered with malaria. I
              came out in 1914 with the Expeditionary Force.
              My nerves are now completely broken down. I
              suffer with pains in the head when I am in the
              line. Sometimes I don't know what I'm doing.

                          *   *   *   *   *   *   *

NICOLA   It's shell shock. He said it all there. His nerves
              are completely broken down. Pains in the head.
              (*She spells it out.*) "I don't know what I'm doing."

MOIRA   If everyone was let off because they claimed
              they didn't know what they were doing, the
              army would be in a sorry state.

NICOLA   But he was ill. Medically ill. And when pushed
              by the court he said . . .

* * * * * *

CHARLES   I knew what I was doing when I left my
                 Battalion, but my nerves were quite broken
                 down. I have not reported sick for my nerves
                 with this Battalion. I did so several times when
                 I was with the 1st and 2nd Battalions. I came
                 out with the first Battalion with the original
                 Expeditionary Force and left it in November
                 1914. I left it wounded. I joined the 2nd Battalion
                 in April 1915. I left it wounded in July 1st 1916.

* * * * * *

MOIRA   See? He admitted he knew what he was doing.

GRAHAM   What about the doctor? What the doctor say?

DANNY   They called his present doctor, who just
                 basically said what Charles said; that he didn't
                 report to him with his nerves.

MAURICE   Maybe he was too nervous.

MOIRA   Oh, for God's sake.

NICOLA   Or maybe the doctor was unapproachable.

GRAHAM   Well they should've got his doctor from his last
                 battalion where he did report sick.

DANNY   It's not easy calling witnesses during war; they
                 could be on leave, they could have been moved
                 to a different country, they could have been
                 injured or killed.

MAURICE   Well they should've got his records, then.

NICOLA   Yeah, they should have, but they didn't.

MAURICE   I bet they did.

NICOLA   Bloody hell, Maurice.

GRAHAM	Look, Nicola, it's getting late, and I've got serious problems going on here.
	(*He tugs at his tutu.*)
MAURICE	He's gonna shit himself again.
GRAHAM	Well thanks for that, Maurice.
MOIRA	Well my mind's made up.
MAURICE	Hey, I must have lost two stone tonight. You should have worn this, Nicola.
NICOLA	(*Furious.*) What?
MAURICE	All those against.
NICOLA	Hang on a minute. Field General Courts Martial in the First World War were ran almost entirely by officers, and when you say officers, you mean public school boys.
MOIRA	Not that "poor northerners at the expense of ignorant generals", again. How tired is that?
NICOLA	It was a class distinction.
MOIRA	Edwardian England *was* a class distinction.
NICOLA	Which doesn't make it right.
MOIRA	But it doesn't make it wrong. It was the way it was.
DANNY	And in 1916 a secret order was given to all officers of the rank of Captain or above, instructing that all cases of cowardice were always to be punished with death.
MAURICE	Rubbish.
DANNY	It's true. Medical excuses were not to be tolerated.

NICOLA   Maybe this is why Charles Kirman's medical
                records were not sent for; maybe the decision
                was already made.

MOIRA   And maybe it wasn't. Maybe they knew he was
                a coward. 'Ang on a minute. Earlier, you said
                he was tried and they gave him one year's hard
                labour and then they changed their minds and
                sent him back to the front.

DANNY   Yes that's right.

MOIRA   So, how many times did he run away?

NICOLA   He was suffering from shell shock.

MOIRA   Danny! How many times did he run away?

NICOLA   He wasn't well.

                (DANNY *looks at* NICOLA.)

MOIRA   Danny!

DANNY   Three times.

GRAHAM   Three times!

MOIRA   What?! Oh my God.

MAURICE   He ran away three times.

MOIRA   Once wasn't enough for him. Not even twice.
                He ran away, abandoned his duty, let down his
                mates, three times.

NICOLA   Cos he was ill.

MOIRA   Cos he was a coward. Go on, Maurice; try
                telling that to your Uncle Walter or whatever
                they call him.

MAURICE   Wilfred.

MOIRA   Him. Try telling Wilfred that some guy who ran
               away, not once but three times, was a little bit
               troubled and see what he has to say. Did he
               ever talk about the people who he lost? His
               mates? Cos my dad did.

NICOLA   You said he never talked about it.

MOIRA   Not when he was sober. But when he was
               drunk, he let it all out. His best mate, who he
               cuddled in his arms and then watched die. Try
               telling the poor bloke who died they're gonna
               honour a deserter.

NICOLA   But the families, they wanted him included.
               The families of Fulstow who had lost boys, they
               knew. God, can you imagine the hurt those
               families must have felt who lost their sons? They
               must have been devastated. Their lives ruined.
               So why didn't they adopt your attitude and
               say, "To hell with him, he was a deserter and
               my son was a hero," and build the memorial
               without his name on it? Why didn't they do
               that? That seems normal. They had more reason
               than most, and that's what you lot want to do.
               I'll tell you why; because in the way that you
               know your dad and your relatives, they knew
               Charles. They knew the family and knew what
               a good lad he was. They said it. If you don't
               include his name then you don't include our
               sons. Now if you want to honour the wishes of
               those parents whose sons died heroes, you have
               to include the name Charles Kirman.

MOIRA   How do we know that?! Is it written down
               anywhere? It's a legend. It's a myth confirmed
               by some bloke in the pub, who no one, apart
               from Nicola Pike, has seen. How convenient is
               that?

MAURICE   Well . . .

MOIRA   Well what? So cowards and deserters, proven
          criminals convicted by a recognized court of
          law, are to be honoured? Is that what you you're
          saying? Well?

MAURICE   It's just –

MOIRA   My father killed himself! (*Pause.*) Oh yes, he
          killed himself because he couldn't deal with
          what he'd been through. And do you know how
          that makes me feel? Do ya? No, you don't. How
          could you?! And you've all got relatives who
          did their bit. You owe it to their memory not to
          allow this. Just think what floodgates this will
          open. I'll not stand by and have you railroad
          some deserter onto a war memorial.

MAURICE   Can we think about it? You know vote
          tomorrow or next week.

GRAHAM   Yeah. It doesn't have to be done now.

MOIRA   Oh yes, it does. And let me remind you, we
          have soldiers now, today, in Iraq, getting injured
          or laying down their lives, God bless them.
          What do you think they'll say? As far as I am
          concerned there is nothing to think about. No,
          we have to do this and do it now, once and for
          all. Those against.

          (MOIRA *raises her hand. There is a pause . . .*
          GRAHAM *slowly and nervously raises his hand.*)

MAURICE   Can I have a bit more time?

MOIRA   No!

MAURICE   (*Pause.*) I'm sorry, Nicola.

          (*He hesitates before slowly raising his hand.*
          NICOLA *looks at them all before walking out
          through the door SL. As she slams the door,
          black out.*)

ACT TWO

Scene One

CHARLES *is in his cell. The SR door opens and* GEORGE JNR, *in military uniform, enters tentatively, carrying a small container. He stands.*

GEORGE JNR   (*Hesitatingly.*) Charlie?

                  (CHARLES *turns and looks at the young soldier, puzzled.*)

                  It's Georgey.

                  (CHARLES *stares for a while. It slowly dawns on him that it's his childhood friend from Fulstow. He is ashamed. He finds it difficult to look at him. Silence.*)

                  I've been transferred. And I heard all about . . .

                  (*Pause.* GEORGE JNR *finds it difficult.*)

                  The Chaplain's outside. (*Nothing.*) He's waiting to come in.

                  (*Pause.*)

                  Look, the lads have donated their rum supplies for you.

                  (*He places the container on the floor behind the sandbags.*)

CHARLES   Well, the truth is, George, I've never had a drink of alcohol in my life – and I don't think I should start now.

                  (*A long pause.* CHARLES *shakes,* GEORGE JNR *is uncomfortable.*)

GEORGE JNR   Shall I get the doctor? He could give you
             something.

CHARLES   No, no I don't want anything. Not tonight,
             George. No, tonight I need to be awake. I need
             to savour every minute. I want to be able to see
             Dora as clear as day. I want to be able to see
             every feature, remember every detail about her;
             her smile, her laughter, her big raucous laughter,
             and that twinkle in her eye and that silly look
             she used to pull with her face when she wanted
             something.

             (*Awkward pause.*)

GEORGE JNR   You've been like a brother to me, Charlie.

CHARLES   Don't say that, George.

GEORGE JNR   You're the greatest person I know.

             (*Awkward.* GEORGE JNR *is unsure about what to
             say or do.*)

CHARLES   I'm gonna rot in hell, aren't I, George?

GEORGE JNR   No. You're not. It's wartime. It's . . . it's what
             it does to people. It . . . distorts things and
             changes things.

CHARLES   Brilliant! Anytime anybody asks anything
             difficult, we get the answer: well, it's wartime.
             It's wartime. You have to expect hardship, it's
             wartime. I went over the top and saw things
             that nobody has a right to see, but that's to be
             expected, isn't it, it's wartime. I had friends,
             mates, screaming in agony begging me to shoot
             them cos they were in so much pain, but that's
             alright, it's wartime. There were thousands
             of casualties yesterday. Oh well, that's to be
             expected, it's wartime. Well I ran away. I did
             it. But that's alright, because it's wartime. But

it isn't, is it? It isn't alright or else I wouldn't
be here. Because all of a sudden they are not
blaming the war anymore, they are blaming
me. It's not the war's fault any more, is it, it's
mine! Or maybe it's hereditary. Maybe it's been
passed down. Maybe I get it from me dad. (*He
remembers his dad.*) Me dad! Oh God, me dad.
I am proud of him, did you know that?

GEORGE JNR   Yeah, I know, Charlie.

CHARLES   Well I don't think I've ever told him. (*Pause.*)
                  When I was little he was a mountain, my dad.
                  He had hands like shovels. He used to pick me
                  up and hold me right above his head and I felt
                  as though I could touch the sky, it was so high.
                  And then he would throw me in the air. Right
                  up in the air. Oh my lord, he used to throw me
                  so high in the air. My heart used to leap into
                  my mouth and for a tiny split second I would
                  be frightened and then at the very last minute
                  he'd catch me. And I would shriek with laughter
                  at the excitement of it all. I couldn't get me
                  breath for laughing. He was a brilliant dad. And
                  I would say, again, again, again, again, again . . .

                  (*He starts to sob.*)

GEORGE JNR   Shall I get the Chaplain?

                  (*There is no reply. Awkwardly,* GEORGE JNR *starts
                  to pray.*)

CHARLES   What ya doin?

GEORGE JNR   I just thought . . .

CHARLES   Stop it. Stop it. Don't pray for me. Don't ask
                  God for anything for me.

GEORGE JNR   He can help.

CHARLES How can He? Cos when I needed Him, He wasn't there. One bullet, that's all I prayed for. One clean bullet and I wouldn't have known anything. But He couldn't give me that, could He? No, no, He gives me this. What sort of a God is that? What sort of God would put anybody through this? They're calling me a coward.

GEORGE JNR You're not. You're not well, Charlie. All the lads have said it. They don't want this. They've seen you change. They know you're ill. They know this is wrong. For God's sake, we were brought out here to shoot the enemy and we're shooting each other. It's not right.

CHARLES Who's gonna do it?

GEORGE JNR What?

CHARLES Who's gonna do it? Who's gonna pull the trigger?

GEORGE JNR Don't do this, Charlie.

CHARLES I need to know.

GEORGE JNR Please, Charlie.

CHARLES Tell me.

GEORGE JNR Nobody wants to do it.

CHARLES (*Shouting.*) Who is going to do it?

GEORGE JNR They're having to draw lots. They're all terrified. They say they're going to shoot to miss.

CHARLES Will you be there?

GEORGE JNR Charlie, please don't.

CHARLES	Will you be there?
GEORGE JNR	No. I can't . . . I just . . .

(*Pause.*)

CHARLES	I'm not gonna wear a blindfold.
GEORGE JNR	What?
CHARLES	I'm not a coward.
GEORGE JNR	No, I know you're not. Everyone knows you're not.
CHARLES	I'm not gonna wear a blindfold. I'm gonna show 'em who's brave. I'm gonna show *some* dignity.
GEORGE JNR	The blindfold isn't for you, Charlie. (*Pause.*) It's for the men who have to do it. And if they have to look you in the eye . . . God knows what that will do to them. Don't put them through that. Please, Charlie.
CHARLES	I have to have some dignity.
GEORGE JNR	Please, Charlie, don't do that to the lads. Don't.
CHARLES	I can do what I fucking want. I don't need a lecture from you or anybody. I think you'd better go. Out! Just fucking get out. I don't need you. Out!

(GEORGE JNR *stands for a while before making his way to the SR door. He checks and looks at* CHARLES *once more.*)

GEORGE JNR	(*With great difficulty.*) Bye, Charlie Farley.

(As GEORGE JNR *exits,* MOIRA GRAHAM *and* MAURICE *explode through the SL door into the committee room.* CHARLES *sobs quietly.*)

Scene Two

Committee Room.

MOIRA   How dare she?! How dare she?!

GRAHAM   There were television cameras and crews
                everywhere.

MAURICE   Sky News, ITV, BBC, they were all there.

GRAHAM   And hundreds of bloody journalists, trampling
                all over the village.

MOIRA   It will have gone all round the world.

GRAHAM   And they didn't care where they parked. They've
                ruined the grass verges. Doreen set the dogs on
                them. And we haven't got any dogs.

MAURICE   What?

GRAHAM   She had me stood behind the door barking.

MAURICE   I didn't even get an interview; they weren't
                interested in me.

MOIRA   We were in all the papers.

MAURICE   I had loads to tell 'em.

MOIRA   And there she was, Nicola Pike, as bold as brass
                on page three.

MAURICE   With her . . .

MOIRA   Don't be so vulgar. It was the *Daily Telegraph*.
                The point is that the vote went against his name
                being included but (NICOLA *enters through SL
                door.*) Nicola Pike completely ignored that and,
                like some modern day crusader, charges off
                and declares to the world his name *is* going to

be included. Who the hell does she think she
is? (*Pause.* MOIRA *becomes aware of* NICOLA's
presence.) You've made this committee a
complete laughing stock.

NICOLA   I don't think so. In fact, it's quite the opposite.
                There has been an amazing amount of support
                for what we are doing.

MOIRA   And what are we doing?

NICOLA   Look, all I did was write one letter to the
                Telegraph. I thought if I got a positive response,
                you might change your mind. But everybody
                else got wind of it and it just snowballed, just
                like that. I'm telling you, all the television
                companies turning up like that was as much a
                surprise to me as it was to you.

MOIRA   And you expect us to believe that.

NICOLA   Did you see the clip of me? I was on the
                morning school run.

GRAHAM   Her hair looked as though it hadn't seen a
                comb. I flagged her down and warned her that
                there were television cameras waiting for her at
                her house. She looked a bugger.

NICOLA   Alright, Graham.

GRAHAM   I even thought there was a bit of a smell . . .

NICOLA   Alright, Graham. Look, if you want, I'll write
                another letter and tell them that there has
                been a terrible mistake and we are not going to
                include Charles Kirman's name after all.

MOIRA   And how is that going to make us look?

NICOLA   But it's not about appearance, is it. It's about
                doing the right thing. It's about the courage of

your convictions. And you do believe it's right
that his name is not included, don't you?

MOIRA   Yes, I do. Very much so.

NICOLA   So you wouldn't mind, would you, if I named
you, in person, as the one who has objected the
most.

(*Pause.*)

MOIRA   It was the committee's decision.

NICOLA   But you are very much against it, aren't you?
You're not embarrassed by the decision you've
made, are you?

MAURICE *I* am.

MOIRA   What?

MAURICE I've been thinking about it.

MOIRA   We've voted twice!

MAURICE I know, (*Imitating* MOIRA.) 'we voted twice'.
But it was late. I was tired. I was dressed as a
rabbit. But I can't sleep now. I've never slept
since that night. I've been thinking of my Great
Uncle Wilfred. And I think he would want
Kirman's name included. I thought this at the
time; I don't know why I didn't say it, but he
always says that many people were termed
heroes because in that split second they were
so terrified they lost control and just went for it.
(*To* NICOLA.) There's something about what you
said, it's been haunting me. I want to change
my vote.

MOIRA   The vote is closed.

NICOLA	That's such a shame, because since all the media coverage there's been some fascinating developments.
MOIRA	Developments?
MAURICE	(*A flash of inspiration.*) They're gonna make a movie . . .
GRAHAM	A movie?
NICOLA	It's not a movie.
MAURICE	I could be in it. I mean, I live here, they love that. Natural, you know. Like *Kes*.
GRAHAM	That was a bird.
MAURICE	No, the boy in *Kes*, he wasn't an actor.
GRAHAM	Well if they are looking for someone who can't act, I think you are the man.
NICOLA	It's got nothing to do with a movie.
MAURICE	What? You missed an opportunity there.
NICOLA	Who did?
MAURICE	You. You. You should have mentioned that when you were on the telly.
NICOLA	I wasn't there to promote a film.
MAURICE	Why not? You can't wait for films to come to you.
NICOLA	Look it's got nothing to do with a movie, alright?! No, since the media exposure, I've been getting letters.
MAURICE	Fan mail?

GRAHAM   It'll be begging letters. That's what happens
              when you're in the public eye.

MAURICE   Cheeky buggers.

GRAHAM   Well they'll get nothing from me, I can tell you.

NICOLA   No, I've been getting letters of support for our
              campaign.

MOIRA   I think we've lost touch of the reality of what's
              going on here. It's not going to happen. I
              repeat, the vote is closed.

GRAHAM   Well I think we should reopen it.

MOIRA   We can't do that.

GRAHAM   We can do what we want. It's important that
              we reach the right decision, whatever that is. I
              was gonna bring this up because when I went
              home that night, like Maurice, I couldn't sleep.
              So I started looking up all this shot-at-dawn
              business. Some of them were young boys, some
              as young as sixteen. Like this lad, what was his
              name? Errm . . . (*He fumbles in his pocket.*) I
              wrote it down. It really bothered me. Herbert
              Burden. He lied about his age. He told them he
              was two years older than he was. And it was
              all too much for him. Ten months later, he was
              court-martialled for running away after seeing
              his friends massacred in a battle. He was shot at
              dawn. He was shot at dawn, still officially too
              young to be in his regiment. And he isn't the
              only one.

NICOLA   There's loads of them. Look at Harry Farr.
              He couldn't hold a pen cos he was shaking
              that much. He tried to see the doctor but was
              told he couldn't see him because he wasn't
              wounded. And the sergeant major – listen to
              this – was *quoted in the court martial papers* as

saying, "If you don't go up the fucking front, I'm
going to fucking blow your brains out." He was
shot at dawn in October 1916.

GRAHAM   It's terrible. And, you know, if they made a
mistake with these then they could have made
a mistake here. And like you said, Nicola, they
are all victims of war.

NICOLA   And they aren't the only ones. I've got a letter
here from two pensioners from London who
say, (*She reads.*) "We've been very touched by
your heart-warming story. Both of our parents
and grandparents were involved in the war and
we know only too well the huge sacrifices they
made. It would make us very happy if you could
accept a small contribution of five pounds
from our pension toward the building of your
memorial." Walter and Enid Shawcross.

MAURICE   Tight buggers.

NICOLA   Maurice!

MAURICE   What?

NICOLA   And I've had one from a company that makes
memorial statues who have offered us one for
free.

MAURICE   We could have a great big one in the middle
of the green with Angels and cherubs blowing
trumpets and water spouting out of the top of it.

GRAHAM   That would do wonders for the shop and the
pub.

MAURICE   I could sing in the pub, songs from the war. (*He
sings 'Lily of Laguna'.*) 'She's my lady love, she is
my love' . . .

GRAHAM   Right, that's it; if he's singing, I'm away.

NICOLA	No, Graham, we can't leave it like this.
GRAHAM	Look, I'd love to stay, but I'm not supposed to be here in the first place. Doreen wants a chat.
NICOLA	What about?
GRAHAM	I don't know, that's what scares me. But let me make it clear. I want to change my vote.

(*He exits through the SL door.*)

MOIRA	Listen, *five* successive governments; *five*, not one, but *five* successive governments have rejected appeals to pardon the soldiers, and the Ministry of Defence refuses to reopen the court martial files, even on the youngest troops.
MAURICE	How do you know all this?
MOIRA	We can all do our research, Maurice. And did you know that John Major told the Commons that pardoning the 'deserters' would be an insult, *an insult*, to those who died honourably on the battlefield and that everyone was tried fairly.
NICOLA	But I'm not talking about everybody. I know there were murderers and skivers who ran away. I know that. But I'm not talking about them; I'm talking about Charles Kirman, from our village. I know he was innocent.
MOIRA	There's no proof of that.
MAURICE	And if we play our cards right, there's money to be made.
NICOLA	Look, Maurice, before you get too excited about the free memorial, I've turned them down.
MAURICE	You've done what?!

MOIRA   You've turned them down?

MAURICE   (*Aghast.*) I'm, I'm, I could, I would. You, you're
               an idiot.

MOIRA   It's not your decision to make. In fact, the more
               this goes on, the more I'm convinced it's merely
               an ego trip.

NICOLA   I'm sorry you think like that. I really am. I
               thought you knew me better than that. I didn't
               want to be on the telly. But what choice did I
               have? They just turned up and thrust a camera
               up my nose. All I want is that memorial built
               with Charles's name on it. (*A beat.*) And your
               approval for that, well it would mean a lot to
               me.

MOIRA   Well you'll never get that.

NICOLA   Well that's a shame. I know you suffered
               terrible with your dad. And I'm sorry for that. I
               really am. But can't you see the similarities? You
               see, your dad couldn't cope in the same way
               that Charles Kirman couldn't cope. But your dad
               survived the war and Charles didn't.

MOIRA   Do you not think I haven't thought of that? Ever
               since you brought this blessed business up I've
               thought of nothing else.

NICOLA   I'm sorry, Moira. I really am. You see, they're
               not so different, Charles and your dad, and we
               can't forget them. We mustn't forget them. *All*
               of them! And you know, since we've started
               this, everywhere I turn I see war memorials. I go
               to places I've been to a hundred times and I say,
               "Oh bloody hell, there's a memorial". But some
               of them are in a dreadful state; they've never
               been touched for years. And people walk past
               'em and don't even give them a second thought.

MAURICE   That's why we need angels and cherubs.

NICOLA   Or there's those that get polished up once a
               year so that councillors and politicians can turn
               up and pretend they care. But I don't want that.
               I want so much more.

MAURICE   Something bigger.

NICOLA   (*Pause.*) I want this memorial to be loved. What
               I am trying to say is, that that will happen if
               it belongs to our village, and the people in
               our village are proud of it, and they can see
               that, after eighty years, they have done a good
               thing. It means something to them and they've
               helped raise the money to install it. It's not
               about films or fame or making money or some
               kind of tribute Disneyland. I like this village. I
               like it just the way it is. It has barely changed
               in the last eighty years and I like it like that.
               No, we are gonna have our memorial and it's
               going to be right, and it's gonna be small and
               tasteful, and it's going to mean something. And
               we are going to bring those ten boys home.
               (*A long silence.*) This isn't about me. It's about
               us – and doing what's right. And we might still
               need you, Moira, to run a cake stall or organise
               the memorial service and we might need you,
               Maurice, to organise a karaoke night in the *Keys*
               to raise money.

MAURICE   Yes, I see where you're coming from, there.

NICOLA   Moira?

MOIRA   If everyone's changed their vote, I don't appear
               to have a choice.

NICOLA   Thank you.

Scene Three

Lights. Music – the ominous sound of drums. Wind is also heard.
Charles Kirman in his cell DSR, stands. An Officer in a greatcoat,
and George Jnr appear from the wing SR. The cast make their
way to SL, turn and face a chair centre stage. Lights up on
Charles Kirman in his cell. The cast sing "Benedictus" by Karl
Jenkins as Charles walks across to DSC, turns, walks up to the
waiting chair, turns and faces DS.

Officer	*Benedictus,*
Nicola	*Benedictus,*
All	*Qui venit in nomine Domini.*
Charles	I'm sorry, sir. I'm sorry, boys.

(*Charles sits on the chair. The Officer marches*
to centre stage. He ties Charles' hands behind
his back, marches round to the front and
stands.)

Nicola   *Hosanna in excelsis*
                  Hosanna in excelsis

(*The cast hum "Benedictus" as one cast*
member reads the last rights.)

Cast Member   In the name of our Lord Jesus Christ
                  I lay my hands on you, Charles Kirman
                  May the Lord in his mercy and love uphold you
                  by the grace and power of the Holy Spirit.
                  May he deliver you from all evil,
                  give you light and peace,
                  and bring you to everlasting life.

                  Dust you are and to dust you shall return.
                  All of us go down to the dust,
                  yet weeping at the grave we make our song:
                  Alleluia, Alleluia, Alleluia.

(*The* OFFICER *proffers a blindfold to* CHARLES.
CHARLES *looks to the troops before deciding. He
looks back to the officer and gives him a nod
of approval. The officer blindfolds* CHARLES *and
then places a piece of white cloth over his heart
before marching away SL. He turns and stands.*)

CHARLES   What's my dad going to say?

(CHARLES *braces himself. The firing squad rifles
peal out and* CHARLES *slumps in his chair.*)

ALL   *Hosanna in Excelsis*
                 Hosanna in Excelsis
                 Hosanna in Excelsis
                 Hosanna in Excelsis

OFFICER   *Benedictus,*

ALL   *Benedictus,*
                 Qui venit in nomine Domini.

(GEORGE JNR *steps in towards* CHARLES. *The cast
slowly exit, singing. A pause.* GEORGE JNR *slowly
unties the blindfold.* CHARLES *releases his arms,
stands, and faces* GEORGE. GEORGE JNR *smiles at
him.* CHARLES *exits USR.* GEORGE JNR *breaks down
and weeps openly.*)

Scene Four

Lights up on the Community Centre. NICOLA *and* MAURICE *burst
into the room through the SL door.* NICOLA *removes the CS chair.*
GEORGE JNR *turns and exits into the wings SR.*

NICOLA   What do you mean, the leaflets haven't come?

MAURICE   I ordered them.

NICOLA   But we're on, on Sunday.

MAURICE   I know.

NICOLA   Did you ring them up?

MAURICE   Yes!

NICOLA   What did they say?

MAURICE   They said they're on the way.

NICOLA   You didn't order them in time, did you?

               (GRAHAM *enters through the SL door. He is
               dressed in full lycra cycling outfit. He removes
               his helmet and hangs it on the back of the door,
               before marching DSR.* NICOLA *watches, agog.*)

NICOLA   Where've you been?

GRAHAM   I've had the worst week of my life.

NICOLA   Oh well, that's where we're different, cos
               mine's been one big bloody bed of roses.

GRAHAM   Apparently the answer to the question, "Can
               you see any grey hairs?" is no. (*A beat.*)
               Sometimes I think we'd be better off if we were
               divorced. She hasn't spoken to me for two
               weeks.

MAURICE   Hey, I'd hang on to her; women like that are
               very hard to find.

NICOLA   We have a flag from the Lincolnshire regiment
               to cover the memorial. When Is Doreen
               dropping off the table decorations?

GRAHAM   I dunno.

NICOLA   Well find out.

GRAHAM   She hasn't spoken to me for two weeks.

NICOLA   Oh, for God's sake. It's like dealing with a
              group of infants. Right, *I'll* ring her. Major
              Woods is going to be the British Legion
              representative. Right, here's the next problem
              you lot won't help me with. I want to get one
              young lad for every young lad's name on the
              memorial. Any ideas?

              (*Nothing.*)

              Brilliant. Right, what about the *Keys* football
              team?

GRAHAM   They won't do it.

NICOLA   How do you know?

GRAHAM   For one, they're a pack of wasters and secondly,
              they are playing the semi-final of the cup on
              Sunday.

NICOLA   They can cancel it.

GRAHAM   Don't be so bloody stupid.

NICOLA   They might.

GRAHAM   They've never been to the semi-final of
              anything before. It's a miracle they've got there
              this year and there's not a hope in hell of them
              cancelling that match.

NICOLA   You're so bloody negative.

MAURICE   Negative.

NICOLA   You do nothing but bloody moan –

MAURICE   Moan all the time.

NICOLA   We'll, I've had enough of it.

MAURICE	So have I.
NICOLA	There's everyone trying to make this work and you, you just knock every bloody idea.
MAURICE	Every bloody idea.
NICOLA	Maurice!
MAURICE	What?
NICOLA	Shut up.
MAURICE	Alright, God.
NICOLA	Twenty pounds says they will.
GRAHAM	You're on.
MAURICE	Who's doing the catering?
NICOLA	Moira.
MAURICE	No, seriously, who's doing the catering?
NICOLA	Moira is doing the catering.
MAURICE	But I thought we intended to eat it.
NICOLA	Moira, with the help of Doris, Winnie and the gang, are doing the catering. Betty Wallis, the sister of Tom Marshall who died in the Second World War, is going to do the official opening. And I'm going to ask Danny to make a speech.
MAURICE	Woah, woah, woah, woah. Hello.
NICOLA	What?
MAURICE	I love making speeches.
NICOLA	I know, but –

MAURICE   Ah! No buts. Speeches are my forte. I am
             President of the Fulstow Operatic Society.
             What's Danny got that I haven't?

GRAHAM   A twenty-eight inch waist.

NICOLA   Danny's doing the speech, and that's the end of
             the matter. Did the television company get back
             to you?

MAURICE   Television?

GRAHAM   They said they're gonna try.

MAURICE   Maybe I should sing a song.

GRAHAM   This is going to be a tasteful do.

MAURICE   Not if Moira's cooking, it's not. Oh come on,
             if she's doing the food then I can sing a few
             songs.

GRAHAM   It'll be a pantomime.

MAURICE   Oh no it won't.

GRAHAM   Oh yes it will.

MAURICE   Oh no it won't.

NICOLA   Oh bloody hell, we've stooped that low, have
             we? Right, stop it. Alright, I know this is a
             mistake – you can sing one song.

GRAHAM   Nicola!

             (*Unnoticed,* TIM *enters through the SL door and
             stands. Eventually* NICOLA *notices him.*)

NICOLA   Tim.

             (*A long, awkward silence.*)

What?

GRAHAM   Right, I'll go and chase the tele up? Tim.
              (*Motioning to* MAURICE.)

TIM   Graham

GRAHAM   Maurice. Maurice!

MAURICE   Oh right.

              (MAURICE *and* GRAHAM *exit through the SL door.*)

TIM   Toby's not doing his homework and he's falling
              behind with his schoolwork.

NICOLA   Oh shit. Oh no, I'm sorry, I forgot. I've just been
              so busy . . . You went? But I thought you were
              snowed under.

TIM   Some things are more important.

NICOLA   (*Pause.*) I'll go and see the teachers next week.
              We'll form a plan to get him back on track.

TIM   It's not a plan he needs.

NICOLA   Look, I'll make it –

TIM   Stop! Stop now! I don't want promises you can't
              . . . or won't keep. The careers teacher was
              there. Piers has been to see him. He's got an
              interview with the R.A.F. fellas in a couple of
              weeks' time. (NICOLA *is visibly shocked. A long
              silence.*) But he wants to make sure it's all right
              with you.

NICOLA   I'll go and see him.

TIM   No, not now. I told him you'd talk to him next
              week when this bloody thing's finished.

(*Pause.*)

NICOLA   I've been thinking maybe we could go on a little
                  weekend away. Have a picnic. You, me and the
                  kids. You know, like we used to. I'm gonna pack
                  it all in. Once Sunday's out of the way, that's it;
                  I'm gonna have no more to do with it. I know
                  you've heard it before, but this time I mean it. I
                  promise.

TIM   He thinks you're going to go off it, ya know? (*A
                  beat.*) No, he knows you're gonna go off it. Just
                  remember, he's growing up. He's growing up
                  hard.

                  (TIM *goes to exit through the SL door.*)

NICOLA   Where are you going?

TIM   Home.

                  (*He exits.* NICOLA *chases after him.*)

NICOLA   Tim, not like this. Tim!

                  (DORA *enters through the SR door. She looks
                  tired. She carries a basket of washing, makes
                  her way DSL, places the basket on the floor,
                  takes out items of washing, folds them and
                  places them on the small table.*)

                          Scene Five

GEORGE JNR, *in uniform, enters through the ajar SR door. He closes
it behind him. He removes his hat and smoothes down his hair.*

GEORGE JNR   Hello, Dora.

DORA   (DORA *is pleasantly shocked.*) George! Oh,
                  George.

(She moves quickly over to him and embraces him. She puts him at arms length and takes him in.)

Oh George, it's so good to see you. *(She moves him over to the table.)* Come in. Come in. Can I get you a cup of tea?

GEORGE JNR   No, I'm fine, thanks.

(They sit. An awkward silence.)

DORA   You look well.

GEORGE JNR   Thanks. It's good to be home for a while. How are you, Dora?

DORA   Oh, well that's not an easy question to answer, George. I go on. I have to for the children's sake. They're getting bigger and stronger by the day. *(Pause.)* I miss him, George. I miss him terribly.

GEORGE JNR   We all do, Dora.

DORA   He thought the world of you, George.

GEORGE JNR   He did more for me than he ever knew.

DORA   I keep imagining that they've made a mistake, got it wrong and that he'll come walking in that door, pick me up and swing me round like he used to. It couldn't be a mistake, could it? I mean, there were loads of men out there. *(Pause.)* Bloody war. Is it ever gonna end? You look after yourself, George. Don't let them get you.

GEORGE JNR   Don't worry about me, Dora.

DORA   Charlie said that to me. *(Pause.)* I got a letter from this commanding officer. But it didn't say

anything. It was very short, it just said that he
was killed in action. How cold is that! I don't
understand it, George. When Elizabeth Sherroff
and Annie Harrison got word of their boys, their
commanding officers went on at length, paying
glowing tributes, but Charles' letter was, well it
didn't say anything, really.

GEORGE JNR   (*Pause.*) Well things have been pretty hectic of
                late; they're expecting a big push any minute
                and well, maybe he had more pressing matters.

                (*Pause.* GEORGE JNR *plucks up the courage.*)

                I was with him when he died.

DORA   Were you, George?

GEORGE JNR   Yeah. He was a hero, Dora.

DORA   Oh, George!

GEORGE JNR   (*Pause.*) We had gone over the top and Charles
                was, well you know Charles, he was as
                determined as ever.

DORA   (*Through the tears, forcing a smile.*) Yes, yes he
                was, he was.

GEORGE JNR   Well, he got hit a couple of times, but it
                didn't deter him. He just went on and on until
                eventually . . . He was courageous to the end.

DORA   I knew it. I just knew it.

GEORGE JNR   I knelt down beside him and held his head. And
                then he spoke.

DORA   (*Gasps.*) Oh!

GEORGE JNR   With all the noise and commotion it was
                difficult to hear, but he said, "Dora." I'm sure he
                said, "Dora."

DORA   (*Singing.*) *I know she loves me,*
                Because she said so.

                I'm sorry, George.

                (DORA, *overcome, exits through the SL door.*
                GEORGE JNR *stands and looks after her. He*
                replaces his cap and makes his way to the door
                SR as FRANCIS *bursts into the room through the*
                SL, door hotly followed by GEORGE MARSHALL
                SNR.)

GEORGE SNR   Francis. Francis. Wait.

                                Scene Six

FRANCIS   He had no right to say that.

GEORGE SNR   I know.

                (GEORGE JNR *exits.*)

FRANCIS   And if anybody else calls my son a coward,
                they will get the same.

GEORGE SNR   It was a good punch, Francis.

FRANCIS   There's plenty more where that came from.

GEORGE SNR   I've never seen a punch like it.

FRANCIS   You go in and tell them in there, if anybody
                calls my son, they will have me to reckon with.
                If they call my son, then they call me. In fact I'll
                tell them myself.

(FRANCIS *marches back into the meeting,* GEORGE SNR *blocks his way.*)

GEORGE SNR	Francis. Francis.
FRANCIS	No, to hell with it, George.
GEORGE SNR	No, Francis, Francis.
FRANCIS	I'll give 'em bloody coward.
GEORGE SNR	It'll do no good. The war is over, Francis. It's been over for over a year.
FRANCIS	I'll bloody take them all on, each and every one of 'em.
GEORGE SNR	Francis, please, Francis. You've made your point loud and clear. You knocked him clean off his feet. I understand how you feel. Many people are with you.
FRANCIS	I shouldn't have come. This was a mistake.
GEORGE SNR	I'm only pleased that you did. Nobody sees you any more. My Lucy has visited Eliza many times and she won't see her.
FRANCIS	She won't see anyone.
GEORGE SNR	But we want to help, Francis.
FRANCIS	Well then, stay away and leave us be. If you want to have a memorial that's fine, go ahead, but just leave Charles and my family out of it.
GEORGE	I'll never do that.
GEORGE SNR	You've no choice. People don't want his name included and that's fine by me. It doesn't matter. They can stick their memorial. It doesn't mean anything and it won't bring my boy back.

No, they can stick it. It'll be forgotten about
in a few years, anyway. It'll just be another
untended headstone in the graveyard. Who'll
remember in ten, twenty, a hundred years? No
one! And that's fine by me, because we don't
want your pity. We can deal with this on our
own.

(FRANCIS *goes to exit.*)

GEORGE SNR   (*Calling out in frustration.*) You're not the only
man to have a lost a son, Francis, don't forget
that.

(FRANCIS *stops and turns.*)

Do you think it's easy for me? Do ya? Cos I'll
tell you now, I cry every day, Francis, and I
don't care who hears it. I'm a grown man and
I weep like a baby. His mother sits in his room
for hours on end staring into space. She lives for
the day she dies so she can be with him again.
Our lives are ruined. We find some comfort
talking to people who are going through the
same. It helps, not much, but it helps. Because
only they know what it feels like. Only they
know the emptiness, the loneliness, the sadness,
the bitterness and anger that we all feel.

FRANCIS   You never mentioned shame, George. You
mentioned a lot of emotions, but you never
mentioned shame. You never mentioned
being pointed at, or people crossing the street
when they see you coming, or a room full of
chattering people falling silent the moment
you enter. You never mentioned the shame of
a daughter-in-law that was unable to collect
a war pension. The shame of having been so
desperate for money that she had to go back
to live with her parents in Southsea. You never
mentioned the pain of having grandchildren that

we don't see. The pain of never seeing the only thing that reminds us of Charles.

GEORGE SNR   I want to help, Francis.

FRANCIS   You never mentioned having a son in jail waiting to be shot by his own men. You never mentioned that. You never mentioned regret and the torture that we live through every day, that somehow we let our boy down. We got it wrong. We failed him. You never mentioned that, because your son died an honourable death.

GEORGE SNR   And so did yours.

FRANCIS   Honourable! Being shot by the very men he fought alongside. I am tortured every day thinking of my boy spending all night in prison knowing that at the first sign of light he was going to be shot. I can't get that image out of my head. What did he go through? Did he deserve that? Does anybody deserve that? We wouldn't treat animals like that. (*A pause.*) I just want to cuddle him and tell him it's all right.

             (FRANCIS *turns to exit.*)

GEORGE SNR   Well, if Charles Kirman's name is not on that memorial then George Marshall's won't be, and that's the truth of the matter.

             (FRANCIS *stops and turns.*)

             George idolised Charles. He was like a brother to him. He was a fine man, and I'll not have anybody say any different. I've spoken to the other families, Francis, and they feel the same. If there are not ten names on that war memorial then there will be no war memorial. I give you my word on that.

(GEORGE SNR *turns and exits back into the
meeting through the SL door.* FRANCIS *stands
awhile. As he exits into the wings SR,* NICOLA,
*carrying a container full of bunting, enters
through the SL door, followed by* MOIRA.)

Scene Seven

NICOLA

I hope people come.

MOIRA

What, do you think people might not come?

(DANNY *enters hurriedly through the SL door. He
mouths to* NICOLA. MOIRA *busies herself, putting
up the bunting.*)

DANNY

I've lost my voice.

NICOLA

What?

DANNY

(*Pointing to his throat.*) I've lost me voice.

MOIRA

People might not come.

NICOLA

You've lost your voice? (*He nods.*) What do you
mean, you've lost your voice? You can't lose
your voice, you've got a speech to make.

DANNY

(*He mouths.*) Sorry.

NICOLA

Never bloody mind sorry. You've had one job to
do. Well sod off in the kitchen and peel some
potatoes. I need a drink.

MOIRA

Morning, Danny.

DANNY

(*Speaking normally.*) Morning Aunty Moi–

(NICOLA *and* MOIRA *snap turn to look at him. He
freezes for a second before hightailing it out.*)

NICOLA   I don't believe this. The little shithouse.

                (NICOLA *produces a hip flask out of her handbag
                and takes a swig.*)

MOIRA   Well that's not going to help, drinking at this
                time in the morning, is it?

NICOLA   I had four gins before I left home. And that was
                seven o'clock this morning. Who's gonna do the
                speech now?

MOIRA   (*Annoyed.*) Well it doesn't matter who's going to
                do it, cos there's going to be nobody here.

NICOLA   Maurice was supposed to leaflet every house.
                He hasn't done it, has he? (*A pause.* NICOLA
                *weighs up the moment and then decides to
                speak.*) Moira . . . while there's just the two
                of us, I want you to know that I couldn't have
                done this without you.

MOIRA   There was more than just me.

NICOLA   No. I can trust you to get things done. And I
                want you to know that I appreciate it.

MOIRA   Thanks, that's kind. And big of you to say. I
                know how hard that must have been. Oh, and
                while we're on. Good news. We've had a letter
                from McDonagh's about the roof. I don't know
                how you've done it, but they've agreed to come
                and discuss the nitty gritty at a meeting on
                Wednesday.

                (*Pause.*)

NICOLA   Ah, right, listen, Moira, I think you could handle
                that now.

MOIRA   What?

NICOLA   You're right, I do too much. I interfere too
              much. And you're more than capable of
              handling the McDonaghs.

MOIRA   No, no, I can't do that. Not now. This is your
              baby.

NICOLA   But I promised Tim that I would be finished
              after today.

MOIRA   No. You've got to see this through to the end.

NICOLA   I'll give you all the help you need. I'll be at the
              end of the phone. Please, Moira.

MOIRA   You gave your word, remember. You can't go
              back on that now.

              (*Pause.*)

NICOLA   Let's talk about this later.

MOIRA   You gave your word.

NICOLA   Let's talk about this tomorrow. And I would
              appreciate it if you didn't mention it.

              (MAURICE *enters through the door SL.* NICOLA
              pursues him across the stage towards SR.)

              You were supposed to leaflet every house. And
              you didn't do it. Come here.

MAURICE   I did. I did. I leafleted everywhere.

              (NICOLA *stops.*)

NICOLA   If no-one comes to this unveiling, I swear, I'll
              castrate you, you bastard.

MAURICE   What have I done?

NICOLA   What's that?

MAURICE	It's a beer glass. I have to take it back to the pub. Me great uncle Wilfred was with us before Christmas last year, and he came back from the pub with his glass. I've been meaning to take it back.

(NICOLA *exudes a smile of recognition.*)

NICOLA	Oh, for God's sake.
MOIRA	Oh bloody hell, the ovens aren't on.

(MOIRA *exits through the SR door.* MAURICE *helps to erect the bunting.* GRAHAM *enters through the SL door and makes his way down to the table DSL. He wears his cycling helmet and cycling clips.*)

Where've you been?

GRAHAM	It doesn't start until half past.
NICOLA	Yes, but the magic fairies don't set it up, do they?
GRAHAM	Right, what do you want me to do?
MAURICE	Get this room sorted.
NICOLA	Clear this lot.

(MOIRA *enters hurriedly through SR door.* GRAHAM *starts to move the DSL table and chairs US to the SL of the sideboard, before helping to put up the bunting.*)

MOIRA	Right, ovens are on.
NICOLA	All we need now is someone to read Danny's speech.
MOIRA	Well, Nicola, you'll have to do it.

NICOLA	I can't do it. You're good at this sort of thing; you do it.
MOIRA	Shall I do it while I'm serving the potatoes or the carrots?
MAURICE	Hello.
GRAHAM	No.
MAURICE	I'll make up a speech.
N / M / G	You bloody won't.
MAURICE	Well who else is gonna do it?
	(*Pause.*)
NICOLA	Right, here. (*She hands him* DANNY'S *speech.*) Just read it. No ad-libbing and no jokes.
	(MAURICE *takes the speech and exits through the door SL.*)
MOIRA	It's nearly ten thirty
NICOLA	Is the bugler here?
GRAHAM	Well there's some spotty sixteen-year-old with a bugle, but whether or not he is a bugler remains to be seen.
MOIRA	Is the football team here?
NICOLA	They're not coming. I offered 'em four pints each but they just laughed at me.
GRAHAM	I did try to tell you.
NICOLA	Graham, not now, for God's sake.
GRAHAM	What did I say?

NICOLA	Graham!
GRAHAM	But you wouldn't listen.
NICOLA	Graham! Will you just fucking shut it, for once.
MOIRA	I've spent months preparing this, and for what?

(TIM *enters through the door SL and stands. The others notice him.*)

NICOLA	Shit, is that the time? Right, everybody get out. Wait for me in the foyer. Just give me a minute. Go on, go.

(MOIRA *chunters as she exits through SL door.*)

MOIRA	It's the last time I get involved in anything like this.
GRAHAM	There's no need to go speaking to people like that.

(GRAHAM *exits through SL door.*)

NICOLA	You've come.
TIM	Did you really think I wouldn't come?
NICOLA	I know how awkward you can be.
TIM	Do the words kettle and black mean anything to you?
NICOLA	I've been a nightmare, haven't I?
TIM	Worse than that.
NICOLA	Why don't you just give me a smack?
TIM	I daren't. You might hit me back.

(*They laugh.*)

The kids are here.

NICOLA   Where?

TIM   They're outside. (*A beat.*) They're in uniform.
             They want to pay their respects. They want to
             lay a wreath. (*Silence.*) They want to know if it's
             alright.

NICOLA   Let me talk to them.

TIM   Not now, there's not time. Anyway, you've got
             enough on. I'll tell 'em. (*A beat.*) Well then?

NICOLA   (*Pause.*) Tell them that nothing would make me
             more proud than to see my boys in their cadet
             uniforms paying their respects. Tell them (*She
             fights her emotions.*) I'm very proud of them.

             (TIM *cuddles her.*)

TIM   Ey, come here.

NICOLA   I don't think I can do this. It's all too much.

TIM   What you talking about? Course you can. Don't
             start going sloppy on me, you silly sod.

NICOLA   Shurrup.

TIM   You shurrup.

NICOLA   You shurrup.

TIM   Right, I'd better get out there; it'll be starting
             soon. Go get 'em, tiger.

             (*She growls.* TIM *walks to the door SL.*)

NICOLA   Tim. (*He checks.*) Thanks.

TIM   What for?

NICOLA   Everything.

TIM   Bugger off.

                (*He smiles and exits. NICOLA has a quick swig
                of her hip flask, realises it's empty, takes
                another one out of her other pocket and
                takes an almighty drink, emptying it one. She
                takes a deep breath and exits through the SL
                door. MOIRA, NICOLA, GRAHAM and MAURICE
                enter, chuntering and bickering from the
                wings SL. NICOLA carries a microphone stand.
                Intermittently, they each notice the gathered
                crowd and freeze. They are taken aback; the
                street outside the Community Hall is heaving
                beyond their wildest dreams. Over three
                hundred people are there. NICOLA is overcome.*)

NICOLA   Shit!

MAURICE   I feel sick.

GRAHAM   There must be three hundred.

MOIRA   I've only catered for seventy-five.

NICOLA   Shit.

GRAHAM   How far did you leaflet?

MAURICE   Look over there.

GRAHAM   Where?

MAURICE   Over there, coming down the street. It's the
                football team.

NICOLA   (*Overcome.*) Oh my God!

MOIRA   They've all got their suits on.

GRAHAM   They've cancelled the match.

MOIRA	Don't they look smart?
GRAHAM	They've cancelled the bloody match.
NICOLA	I could bloody eat 'em, each and every one of them.
GRAHAM	I owe you twenty and I'm bloody glad.
NICOLA	No you don't. Keep it. They're bloody here.
GRAHAM	Are you crying?
MAURICE	No.
GRAHAM	You are.
MAURICE	I'm not.
GRAHAM	You are, you're bloody crying.
MAURICE	(*Breaking down.*) I can't help it.
GRAHAM	Here, for God's sake.
	(MAURICE *takes the handkerchief and blows hard on it, wipes the tears from his eyes and tries to console himself.* NICOLA *places the microphone stand DSC.*)
NICOLA	Maurice. Go on.
	(MAURICE *looks to audience and freezes.*)
MAURICE	(*Pause.*) I can't.
NICOLA	What?
MAURICE	I can't do it.
NICOLA	What?! Oh my God!

(NICOLA, *shocked and desperate, snatches the speech off* MAURICE, *makes her way to the microphone stand. She is terrified. She turns back for support, and* MOIRA *and* GRAHAM *encourage her. She approaches the microphone.*)

Oh heck.

(*She tries to address the audience but is intimidated by the microphone. She moves it out of the way.*)

I can't do this.

(*She lifts the speech up to read it, but thinks better of it.*)

I can't read this, I'm sorry.

(*She hands the speech back to* MAURICE *and addresses the audience once more. Pause.*)

I wasn't supposed to be doing this. It was supposed to be somebody else. Right. (*Pause.*) Err . . . oh God . . . I know that most of you here are family people. Let me ask you this. Do you love your son? (*A beat.*) Do you love your husband? (*A beat.*) Do you love your dad? Do ya? Cos I do. I love them with all of my heart. And if anything happens to them, it hurts me more. It hurts me more than words can say. I don't know whether it's a mam thing, or a woman thing or a family thing, but I want more for them than I do myself. (*Pause. She takes in the audience and nervously carries on.*) When my eldest son was about four or five I lost him – in a shop. I'd turned me back for a minute and he was gone. He wasn't there. It was a panic. They made announcements. Everyone was looking for him. He was missing forever. That forever was four minutes. And for four minutes my life stopped. I didn't know who

I was. For four minutes the bottom dropped
out of my world. Well, we found him in the
window playing with some things he'd found.
And I was crying and cuddling him and kissing
him, and he didn't know what was going on. He
probably thought his mum had gone mad. Well
he wasn't wrong. So I can't begin to imagine
what it must be like to lose my boys . . . (*She
fights her emotion.*) In fact I can't go there. I
can't even think about it. But when these boys
were called, they didn't flinch. They did their
duty; what they thought was expected of them,
by their family, by their King – and by their
country. Brave people each and every one of
them. This memorial is but a tiny, tiny, tiny way
of saying thank you. Thank you to the boys,
thank you to the mams and dads and sisters
and families who experienced, well, well, such
unbelievable grief so that my kids can run free
and dream of a wonderful future. When you
look at it, think of your family and think, thank
God for the bravery of these boys and their
poor, poor families. And when you go home, go
and give your family a cuddle and tell them you
love them. Cos that's what I'm gonna do. No
regrets. Thank you.

(GRAHAM, MAURICE *and* MOIRA *step forward.*)

GRAHAM   The ten Fulstow boys of World War One.
                Private Arthur West.

MAURICE   Private George Sutton Taylor.

MOIRA   Private Tom Wattam.

GRAHAM   Private Albert S. Sherriff.

MAURICE   Private Herbert Harrison.

MOIRA   Private Charles H. Kirman.

GRAHAM   Private Harold Pennell.

MAURICE   Rifleman Herbert E. Green.

MOIRA   Private George Marshall.

GRAHAM   Private Charles Hyde.

MAURICE   And in the Second World War: Private Marjorie
                Sutton.

MOIRA   Private Viola Wells.

GRAHAM   Gunner Tom Marshall.

MAURICE   Sergeant Claude Marriott.

MOIRA   Trooper J. Stanley Maddison.

                (*As the* BUGLER *plays the last post, he hits
                a few bum notes and the cast, somewhat
                embarrassed, simultaneously and slowly turn
                their heads to look left.*)

MOIRA   I've only catered for seventy-five.

GRAHAM   Moira, why don't you cheer up and stop being
                so miserable.

                (*The cast, quite astonished, very slowly turn
                their heads to look at* GRAHAM.)

NICOLA   Maurice, your song.

MAURICE   What?

NICOLA   Your song.

                (MAURICE *beams with delight*)

MAURICE   What? Oh right.

(MAURICE *retrieves the microphone and places it CS.* GRAHAM *collects his banjo.* GRAHAM *plays and* MAURICE *starts to sing.*)

MAURICE

She's my lady love,
She is my dove, my baby love,

+ GRAHAM

She's no gal for sitting down to dream,
She's the only queen Laguna knows;

(MAURICE *and* GRAHAM *back away from the microphone US still singing, albeit quietly.* MOIRA *joins in.* NICOLA *makes her way to the microphone and speaks over their singing.*)

+ MOIRA

I know she likes me.   (NICOLA: *final speech.*)
I know she likes me
Because she says so;
She is ma Lily of Laguna.
She is ma Lily and ma Rose

NICOLA

On the 16th August 2006, nine months after the Fulstow War Memorial was opened, the Defence Secretary, Des Browne, much to the delight of many families, announced that a posthumous pardon was to be awarded to all the three hundred and six soldiers who were shot at dawn during World War One.

(TIM *and* DANNY *enter from the wings SR and SL respectively to join the rest of the cast singing. The last verse of the song is sung unaccompanied, with harmonies, as they all move DS. Lights and bows.*)